PASTORAL CARE OF
GAYS, LESBIANS, AND THEIR FAMILIES

Creative Pastoral Care and Counseling Series

Howard W. Stone, Editor

BOOKS IN THE SERIES

Crisis Counseling (revised edition)
Howard W. Stone

Integrative Family Therapy
David C. Olsen

Counseling Men
Philip L. Culbertson

Woman-Battering
Carol J. Adams

Counseling Adolescent Girls
Patricia H. Davis

Cross-Cultural Counseling
Aart M. van Beek

Creating a Healthier Church
Ronald W. Richardson

Grief, Transition, and Loss
Wayne E. Oates

When Faith Is Tested
Jeffry R. Zurheide

Competency-Based Counseling
Frank Thomas and Jack Cockburn

Pastoral Care of Older Adults
Harold G. Koenig and Andrew J. Weaver

The Pastor As Moral Guide
Rebekah L. Miles

Premarital Guidance
Charles W. Taylor

Pastoral Care of Gays, Lesbians, and Their Families
David K. Switzer

PASTORAL CARE OF GAYS, LESBIANS, AND THEIR FAMILIES

DAVID K. SWITZER

with a concluding chapter by
John Thornburg

FORTRESS PRESS   MINNEAPOLIS

Library of Congress Cataloging-in-Publication Data

Switzer, David K., 1925—
    Pastoral care of gays, lesbians, and their families / David K. Switzer ; with a concluding chapter by John Thornburg.
        p.   cm.
    Includes bibliographical references.
    ISBN 0-8006-2954-X (alk. paper)
    1. Gays—Pastoral counseling of. 2. Homosexuality—Religious aspects—Christianity. 3. Church work with gays. I. Thornburg, John. II. Title.
    BV4437.5.S85 1999
    259'.086'64—dc21   98-48890
                                             CIP

The paper used in this publication meets the minimum requirements of American National Standard for Information Sciences – Permanence of Paper for Printed Library Materials, ANSI Z329.48-1984.

Manufactured in the U.S.A.   AF 1-2954

03   02   01   00   99   1   2   3   4   5   6   7   8   9   10

CONTENTS

Editor's Foreword   vii

Acknowledgments   ix

Introduction   1

1. The Constant Dilemmas of Pastoral Caregiving   5

2. What Is Homosexuality and How Does It Come About?   15

3. What the Bible Says about Homosexuality
   (Homosexual Acts)   37

4. Pastoral Care and Counseling of Gays and Lesbians   65

5. Pastoral Care and Counseling of Families of
   Gays and Lesbians   114

6. The Congregation as a Caring Community for Gay Men
   and Lesbians, by John Thornburg   139

Notes   148

Further Reading and Resources   155

EDITOR'S FOREWORD

In the church and even outside of it, few subjects stir controversy—and tempers—more quickly than the church's response to homosexuality. In *Pastoral Care of Gays, Lesbians, and Their Families*, David Switzer recognizes the sensitivity of the homosexuality issue in the church; his approach to the topic, however, is somewhat different from other recent writings on the subject. Switzer's focus is to help pastors and congregations offer pastoral care to gay and lesbian individuals in their midst.

Switzer believes that pastoral care requires that we go "into situations that may be frightening, the out of the way places, to talk with 'foreigners,' to those of whom many of our church members do not approve, often when we have something else to do . . . when we are very tired, when we feel anxious, when we are not sure how we are going to respond helpfully" (p. 9). The purpose of *Pastoral Care of Gays, Lesbians, and Their Families* is to present a way parish pastors can offer pastoral care to homosexual individuals and their families.

In the first chapter, Switzer immediately tackles some of the obvious dilemmas of pastoral caregiving to homosexuals and their families. How can pastors and lay persons respond in a constructive way to everyone in need regardless of how they feel or what they believe about the other? The pastor's task is to help all parishioners to respond lovingly toward others, even though they do not agree with their actions.

Chapter 2 focuses on what "homosexuality" means. This excellent chapter presents a historical perspective on homosexuality and looks at possible sources of same-sex preference (psychological, biological/genetic, and family systems). The discussion of twin research and homosexuality is especially helpful.

The third chapter addresses the scriptural understanding of homosexual acts. Ministers cannot respond pastorally to homosexual individuals or their families without first considering what various authors in the Bible have to say about homosexual acts. Switzer goes into considerable detail on this point—detail that I believe is necessary if pastoral care is to be responsive to the Word of God.

Chapter 4 focuses on pastoral care and counseling of gays and lesbians. It covers such topics as same-gender couple counseling, coming out, suicide, ministry to persons with AIDS, and ministry to teenagers as well as adults.

The fifth chapter also focuses on pastoral care and counseling, in this case with the families of gay or lesbian individuals. It discusses some of the typical reactions of parents to the "coming out" of a gay or lesbian child and presents ways to help bring about reconciliation.

In the final chapter, *Pastoral Care of Gays, Lesbians, and Their Families* addresses the ministry of the congregation to gays and lesbians. This chapter, written by parish pastor John Thornburg, suggests specific, practical ways in which congregations can extend hospitality and fellowship to gay and lesbian individuals.

This is a thoughtful, reasoned book written by a pastoral theologian with many years of experience in counseling gay and lesbian individuals and their families. It is my hope that *Pastoral Care of Gays, Lesbians, and Their Families* will challenge readers to examine their ministry to gays and lesbians in their congregations and enhance their ministry to them.

HOWARD W. STONE

ACKNOWLEDGMENTS

Where to start?

Probably with Howard Stone, the editor of this series of books, good friend and colleague, who from time to time over a period of several years would say, "I'd surely like for you to do a book for this series." Year after year I would just let the statement pass as one of those things someone might say to a good friend. Besides, I didn't know what I'd do. But the last time he said it, an accumulation of experiences led me to respond, "OK." We discussed the subject. There didn't seem to be a book exactly like it for a clergy audience. So this is it.

Perhaps my greatest debt of gratitude goes to numerous gays and lesbians who over the last fifteen or so years have been willing to share their experiences with me: personal friends who were clergy, psychologists, and others; persons who have come to me for counseling; parents, usually referred by another psychotherapist, who have almost always expressed their pain, confusion, anger, sadness that their own child, whom they had loved and nourished, in whom they had invested themselves, and for whom they'd had such hopes and dreams, was lesbian or gay. All these have taught me much and have touched my deepest feelings. God bless them all.

Then there is Ann Ralston, staff secretary at Perkins School of Theology, Southern Methodist University. Without her knowledge, skill, patience, good spirit, and sense of humor, this book never would have been completed. Imagine typing this material over and over and over again without ever once telling me to get out and never come back. My appreciation cannot fully be expressed.

Finally, I am indebted to my wife, Theresa McConnell, clergywoman, pastoral counselor, social worker, and an amazing emotional support to me "in sickness and in health"; and to my daughter, Rachel McConnell-Switzer, nine years old at this writing, adding significantly to the affection, joy, and fun of our family. And I have definitely needed all of these by both of them.

INTRODUCTION

Why is the subject of ministering to gays and lesbians and their families important enough to be published? It is important because we clergy and other professional workers in the church are committed to serving Christ and because Jesus, as the Christ, was committed to serving any person in any kind of need. That is what the love of *God* means: love in action on behalf of everyone.

It is important for there to be such books as this because there are millions of gay and lesbian persons in the United States (in addition to those in other countries), and even a larger number of millions of close friends and family members of lesbians and gays. The best recent research discovered that the percentage of gay men in the population is 3.7 percent.[1] This is considerably less than the 10 percent stated by a number of speakers and writers, then requoted by their listeners and readers. Those who use this figure refer to an early study by Alfred Kinsey.[2] In fact, Kinsey and his collaborators were investigating sexual *behavior,* as the title of the book makes clear. Kinsey is even more precise as to what he is saying: 10 percent "*more or less* exclusively homosexual [behavior] . . . for at least *three years* between the ages of sixteen and fifty-five" (emphasis mine).[3] That three-year period becomes significant when we realize that 49.6 percent of Kinsey's subjects were or had been incarcerated.[4] Anyone who has been around a bit knows that a fair amount of sexual behavior takes place in prisons in order to reduce sexual tension and/or to establish one's dominance over others. Most of this behavior is done by men who are otherwise clearly heterosexual. A period of three years would certainly include a number of prisoners who would have been included in Kinsey's 10 percent figure.

A later colleague of Kinsey eliminated the prison population from the earlier work and determined that 4 percent of white adult males were predominantly homosexual.[5] After other factors are taken into account, Harry suggests that the figure for all males would raise only slightly the 3.7 percent figure that his survey disclosed. Some writers have estimated that there are fewer lesbians than gay men, and some say there are probably more. I have not yet discovered a scientific study that gives any clear direction toward a fairly accurate figure. Whether the figure for gay men is 3.7 or three or four, more or less, and whether the figure for lesbians is somewhat more or less than that makes no difference to the point to be made here.

In 1995, there were (rounded off to the nearest thousand) 172,194,000 men and women in the United States between the ages of twenty and seventy-four.[6] Taking a conservative estimate of 4 percent for the gay and lesbian occurrence in the population, it would mean that there are approximately 6,887,760 persons of the stated age range in this country who are gay or lesbian, plus some younger and some older. That would mean, in rough estimate, that there may well be at least twenty-three million parents, children, spouses, and brothers and sisters of gays and lesbians. Taken together, we might be talking about a minimum figure of thirty million people, not even counting very close "straight" friends. That would be over 17 percent of our total population between the ages of twenty and seventy-four who are lesbian, gay, and members of their families. This is a vast number of people.

Who are the gays and lesbians, their parents and other relatives, and where are they? Some of them are clergy reading this right now. There are even more who are members of many clergy families. They are many nonordained professional church workers as well. There have been gay bishops and the sons and daughters of bishops. They work alongside of us, live next door to us, are members of the various groups that we belong to, and participate in a number of activities with us. They are friends, and we often are not aware that they are lesbian or gay.

They are attending worship at most churches of all denominations and in synagogues and temples. They are former active church members who for various reasons feel unwanted, rejected, ashamed, and angry as a result of official denominational pronouncements, dogma and doctrine, sermons, and condemnation or ostracizing by individual church members.

A television station made and aired an excellent video about AIDS and put a human face on it. One scene was of a support group of parents here in Dallas whose children have AIDS or who have died of it. In the midst of it, a woman stated: "I used to be active in my church, but I hardly go at all any longer. I feel like such a hypocrite. I know what the leaders of our denomination have said about homosexuals. I feel, you know, like when I go to church I'm supporting those statements. I went once or twice after I found out about my son, but I am not going back."[7]

It is important for there to be books dealing with the pastoral care (including congregational care) of gays and lesbians and their families, because their needs are so great and because so many of them long to be reconciled to God, to the church, and to themselves.

Larry Kent Graham, an ordained minister, pastoral counselor, and seminary professor, went to four major cities in the United States and in each one taped detailed interviews with lesbians and gays. These interviews not only identified several sources of care that the interviewees had received (including clergy and congregation), but also revealed "the capacity of lesbian and gay persons for creative, deep, and loving communion with God."[8]

I was impressed by the large number of those interviewed who had a hunger for a loving relationship with God and for the worship, fellowship, and pastoral care of the church. I was saddened, though not surprised, that many of these spiritually hungry people experienced the church as being closed to who they really are and many clergy as not being understanding—some apparently not willing to try to understand, even seeming fearful of becoming too involved. Yet lesbians and gays are also those whom God loves. We as clergy are those with the potential to confirm and demonstrate that love.

But why am I the one who is writing this book on the importance of pastoral ministry to gays and lesbians and their families and attempting to suggest some specific areas and methods of that ministry? That's a legitimate question that might have occurred to you. First, just to be clear, I am not gay. I am happily married and have two grown married children and one in elementary school.

In the Marine Corps in World War II, my college and seminary years, and my first two parishes (a rural area and a rapidly growing city church), nothing occurred and I read and heard nothing that would even lead me to think about the possibility of the existence of homosexual persons around me. Somewhere in my brain I knew that there were gay and lesbian persons, but I was, with only one exception, unaware of their presence. It was definitely not a "hot topic" in the churches or media of that time.

As a college chaplain for nine years, perhaps a half dozen students talked with me about their homosexual feelings and in a couple of instances confessed their sexual activity. Some of them wanted help in sorting out who they were sexually. I frankly don't know how helpful I was, a terrible but true thing to say about an educated person and one who'd had quite a variety of life experiences.

Then I took a position as Minister of Pastoral Care and Counseling at a large church on the West Coast, where a number of gay men of college and young adult age and one middle-aged man either chose to come to see me or were arrested for sexual misdemeanors and referred to me by the courts. I had already begun as a college chaplain to read some of the available technical books of that time, all of which dealt with the psychotherapy of the "homosexual male" and were based on the origin of homosexuality in the mother/father/child set of relationships. I learned some rudimentary concepts about family systems and psychotherapy from these books, but I learned even more from the gays themselves. Shortly before I left that church, the event I recount in chapter 1 occurred. I began to think, to be more aware, to have a broader, deeper view of pastoral care.

In 1978, Dr. Wayne Oates, editor of a Christian Care series of books, asked if I would write one for parents who have just discovered that a child of theirs of whatever age is "homosexual."[9] By that time I had had numerous pastoral conversations with graduate students who were lesbian or gay, with several minister friends of mine who were gay, and with two women whose minister husbands had revealed to them that they were gay and that they wanted to leave the marriage. The book's appearance led to long distance phone calls from clergy of several denominations who wanted to talk to me about the stress they were under as gay married men with children and pastors of large churches who were trying to control their sexual urges, all the while trying to keep their sexual orientation secret. In addition, as I gave workshops on different topics in other cities, it was relatively frequent that one of the ministers in attendance would ask to speak to me in private and then tell me that he was gay and discussed his agonizing quandary. Letters arrived from distressed parents of young adult gay children. But I learned the most about the pain of these parents when they were referred to me by psychiatrists and psychologists and when I worked to assist them in their grief, anguish, confusion, and anger in the context of their love for their child.

I was struck with this reality all around us that most of the time has been kept under wraps. I was deeply moved by the struggles and anguish of many of the gays and lesbians themselves and had tears with numerous parents who were brokenhearted, did not understand, and felt helpless. I am writing this book in the hope that I can raise the awareness of some clergy, present some information that might help in thinking through this area of responsibility for ministry as it is being increasingly presented to us, touch the compassion that I know pastors have, and perhaps offer something helpful for that ministry.

1

THE CONSTANT DILEMMAS OF PASTORAL CAREGIVING

It has been many years ago now, but the experience is still quite vivid in my memory. I was alone in the parsonage one night, grateful for the time just to read the evening paper leisurely. Naturally, about 8 P.M. the phone rang. A man introduced himself to me as George Edwards (not his real name, of course). He told me that we'd never met, but that he was a member of our congregation. It was a large congregation, so there were quite a number of people I did not know. He wanted very much to talk with me alone. Was it possible that very night? I assured him that it was and settled back down in my chair to wait. In twenty-five or so minutes the doorbell rang.

I opened the door to see a nice-looking, well-built man, probably in his middle forties. After we got seated, George began to talk. He acknowledged once again that we had never met, though he said that he had heard me preach several times and expressed his appreciation for the sermons. As a result of the way he perceived me as a person through my preaching, he said that he believed he could trust me. George told about his marriage to a very good woman whom he loved very much. He went on to describe how over the years they had grown apart. He knew the reason. He was gay and he had never told her this. He wasn't very interested in sex with her, although he loved her, and he was very aware that neither he nor she was sexually satisfied. He had to be constantly on guard in his conversation with her lest the "secret" come out. Finally, in despair over the deterioration of this relationship with someone he really cared about and appreciated, he opened the conversation with her about his awareness of her dissatisfaction with their marriage and the stress that he was constantly feeling, and then he told her that he was gay. She was stunned. Together they discussed their future and after a period of time decided to divorce. They were both heartbroken, though they realized that this was going to be best for both of them.

During the six years since the divorce, he had been terribly lonely. He didn't want to go to gay bars and didn't believe in meaningless, casual sex. He also was guarded in his relationships with men. In the last few months, however, he had been seeing a particular man very frequently. They enjoyed one another and began to love each other. Just recently they had decided to live together as life partners. He said to me, "I've never loved anyone like I do this man. I've never known love could be like this. It's such a new experience. It's wonderful."

During all of this conversation, probably forty to forty-five minutes, I'd been listening very carefully and had attempted to understand what his experience had been like for him, and from time to time I tried to respond in ways that communicated my understanding of his experiences. Apparently nothing I said or did closed him up or shut him out, but rather encouraged him to say more and to be more and more open. I had become increasingly aware that in my sixteen years of ministry, no one had ever told me a story like the one George was telling me. I believe honestly that I wasn't anxious because of his marriage difficulties or his divorce (I had talked about this a number of times with people), or even because he was gay. But I was aware of increasing anxiety as I began to wonder where all this was leading. Why was he telling me this? What was the "punch line" going to be? And how would I respond? This was developing into a pastoral dilemma.

After he expressed the depth of love that he and the other man had for each other and that they had decided to live as life partners, he fell silent for a moment.

As George's pastor, what would you do?
- Just be quiet until he says something else. Maybe he'll say something you can respond to.
- "I'm shocked to think that you'd tell *me* as a *minister* something like that."
- "Have you ever had psychotherapy to try to change to being heterosexual? If not, I know a good psychiatrist and I would be glad to refer you."
- "Well, before you leave, let us pray."
- Think silently to yourself, "Why was I home tonight?"
- "How can you call yourself a Christian? How can you be coming to church regularly? Haven't you read what the Bible says about what you're doing?"
- "Well, I have to go to bed now. Thank you for coming by. Good night."
- "I appreciate your sharing this with me. I wonder if we couldn't make an appointment to meet in my office and talk in more detail about your problem."

Perhaps none of this corresponds with what you would think or say or do. If you were listing possible responses, you could probably think of a number of others to add to these I've just proposed—some of which are serious and some of which are caricatures—while reflecting on the dilemma you would be in, depending on your beliefs, feelings, and experience in pastoral care and counseling. I imagine that all of us would like very much to do something that would be helpful to this man in the light of our commitment to Christ.

(At this point, pause for a moment and think how you might respond when George got to the point of speaking of the wonder of his love for another man, and then fell silent. If you don't choose just to be silent—always an option—make a statement or ask a question. Put this in the exact words that you would use to respond to him.)

As I have mentioned, this was the first time that I had ever had to respond to this sort of situation. As a matter of fact, much of what I had done in pastoral care over the years I had done for the first time. I often didn't know with any certainty the most helpful thing that I as a pastor could say or do in a given situation or in response to a particular statement or question. During the many more years since then, first times still continue to arise with some frequency. We as pastors constantly face dilemmas.

I was in the midst of a dilemma with George that night. Check your response with the one that somehow was given to me. After a brief pause I said something like, "So now that you've told me all of this, what's your reason for doing it?" This type of response (there could of course be a number of different ways of saying it), has the advantage of our not making a *guess* about what he wants and then going on to say something quite off the wall and unhelpful on the basis of our guess. It also has the advantage of inviting him to continue speaking, but with a particular necessary focus. How can we know what to say or do next unless we know a person's motivation for talking about it with us in the first place?

George was quite prepared to respond, and his response had the effect of plunging me right back into another dilemma. "I just wanted to share this with you as my minister, and I wanted to know what you think of me and what I've told you." So *now* how do you respond? Different pastors, different answers.

How could it be otherwise? We believe different things. The families in which we grew up were different, and we had different early life experiences. We have different cultural heritages. Our friends and activities were different as we grew up. Later life experiences were different. We've heard different things about gays and lesbians. We have different feelings about them. Obviously, we as clergy would say things that differ from one another. The dilemma is, how can we be true to the gospel as we understand it, and be most helpful to George and others like him at the same time? In my view it is crucial to keep clear in our minds that this conversation with George is a situation of *pastoral care*. Such clarity will help us have a sharp focus within which several possible helpful responses could be made.

THE ROLE OF PASTORAL CARE IN THE CHURCH

Pastoral care, of course, is only one of a number of essential activities of ministry within the life of the church and for which we as clergy are responsible. Each different function of ministry has its own particular form and procedures, its own usual situations in which it is most appropriate. All are essential to the life of the congregation: worship, preaching, education, pastoral care, outreach of the congregation or a group of congregations to the community in which we live, and other activities that are directed toward growth in faith and the strengthening of the church. Activities comparable to those we today call pastoral care were an integral part of the life of the early church, as were the other activities I have just mentioned.

Look at the story of the Jews, who understood themselves to be called together by God to fulfill God's purposes: the telling and retelling of their history as a people upon whose heads lay the hand of God; their worship of God; the songs and liturgy; the many laws that were designed to distinguish them from other peoples among whom they lived, as well as to teach them what it meant to behave responsibly toward one another and to *care* for one another, especially the poor and the needy; and preaching, or proclaiming the Word of God for concrete historical situations. These were distinguishable aspects of their life together but connected because they were all essential to maintaining the life and witness of the people of God.

Out of this people arose Jesus, who preached, taught, worshiped, healed, and had conversations with people in need. Jesus' relationship with those people, a relationship in which he spoke words of confrontation and forgiveness, revealed the powerful love of God. His words revealed people to themselves in a way that had the potential to stimulate faith and a change of life. These were his acts of pastoral care.

The disciples, following Jesus' death and resurrection, as these are described in the Gospels and in Acts, understood themselves as being called to continue in the world the ministry of Jesus. So they, too, preached, taught, gathered for worship, and reenacted the last supper of Jesus and his disciples, sealing their own unity by their breaking of bread and sharing the cup. Some of the disciples healed, and they all paid attention to the needs of individuals and families and the poor in the church, even organizing themselves by selecting certain persons to see to it that those needs were met.

As the church, and as leaders in the church, we are called upon by our history and by the present Word of God to respond to the needs of the world, our own community of faith, and any and all individuals and families who are in need.

Pastoral care refers to a designated representative of the community of faith, a pastor or a lay person, having a particular type of conversation with a person or small group of persons, at least some of whose needs have the possibility of being met by this conversation and sometimes other acts in this relationship. Most pastoral care is directed toward the developing of a relationship of trust with others at a time of their particular need. This relationship and the focused and disciplined conversation of the caregiver lead to the clarifying of the need that the persons have expressed, perhaps eliciting other related needs, and identifying areas of potential healing and growth, including growth in faith. The caregiver, as a result of his or her quality of personhood, insights, and skills, facilitates the development of this relationship through particular words. His or her words provide the conditions for the greatest possibility of the others' self-exploration, development of insight, increased motivation for change, and decision-making. Particular ways in which we respond to persons will vary somewhat from situation to situation, but the expressions of empathy, open-ended questions, and sometimes confrontation lead to their and our insights into the persons and their situations. Such conversations can clearly be identified as pastoral care.

Obviously, then, the process of pastoral care is not the same process as that of preaching, education, or worship, although the goal of all that we do in all of our functions of ministry is the same: to present the transforming love of God as God is revealed in Jesus the Christ and contribute to the Christian community, that is, deepened faith in God and commitment to God and to one another.

In saying this, it should be clear that pastoral care is not just a set of procedures designed to be simply the means of supporting the proclamation of the Word through preaching, although it *may* do that in some instances. Pastoral care is not merely an adjunct to preaching as proclamation, but in and of itself it *is* proclamation:

> [It] proclaims the Word through faithful servanthood. In this service it reveals something of the quality of the life of the kingdom [of God]. This does not mean that, at appropriate times, pastoral care does not discuss the content of the faith, share the scriptures, or teach an ethical perspective. Of course it does. Yet while pastoral care is one means of *demonstrative proclamation,* it has its own set of procedures designed to produce the unique relationship in which a person in need might experience the love of God, see the servanthood of Jesus through God's present servants, and possibly respond and grow in faith. The procedures and relationships of pastoral care distinguish it from acts of worship, preaching, and teaching, even though all are united in one goal.[1]

Proclamation through pastoral care requires that we too go to the disturbed, into situations that may be frightening, the out of the way places, to talk with "foreigners," to those of whom many of our church members do not approve, often when we have something else to do (that is *always,* isn't it?), when we are very tired, when we feel anxious, when we are not sure how we are going to respond helpfully. But Christ goes with us, and we go in his name.

We don't go *exactly* as Jesus did, as a savior, immediately being able to penetrate the minds of people and have insight into their situations, needs, fears, conflicts, and so on with the power to produce change instantly. Such insight will come to us and to the other persons only slowly as we have been willing as pastors to express frequently and consistently our understanding of what the person has *just* expressed (the communication of empathy), by asking for clarification, by periodic brief summaries of what we've understood to this point, by pointing out any discrepancies in what they might have been saying, and by our willingness to share our own feelings, experiences, thoughts, convictions, and faith at appropriate times so that the other may become more expressive or see things in a different way and gain strength to change. This all demands we *know* clearly these facilitative conditions that we must provide in the growing relationship and the *skill* actually to do so. It also demands patience on the part of the pastor and the other(s).

Of course, in many circumstances, we will need to assist persons to move on to other people who can help meet their need in ways that we can't: psychological or psychiatric professionals, a hospital emergency room, a sheltered workshop, a support group for persons with particular difficulties, a shelter for battered women, etc. In so doing, we do not abdicate our direct pastoral relationship.

There is a final critical point that is also a source of dilemma for us in certain circumstances of pastoral care, with dilemmas varying from pastor to pastor. Jesus was obviously willing to spend time with and act on behalf of *anyone,* and most frequently they were physically and mentally handicapped or social outcasts. We've mentioned them: the Samaritan woman, demoniacs (mentally ill), lepers, a woman who had committed adultery, the Syrophoenician woman whose daughter was possessed by an unclean spirit. So are we in Christian ministry, disciples of Jesus, called to spend time with and serve the comparable contemporary persons in critical need: the "outcasts," "foreigners," the socially criticized and ostracized, the homeless, gays and lesbians, alcoholics and drug abusers, persons with AIDS, and others. Not only do we proclaim the gospel to them by our being with them and being as helpful as we can to them, but we also proclaim to our own congregations or other constituencies that these are whom Christ was concerned about and whom *they* (the congregation, the physicians and other medical personnel, whoever) should also be concerned about, serve, and respect as human beings. The tragedy is, Larry Graham found in his videotaped interview project, that even though some of the lesbians and gays he interviewed found helpful clergy and supportive congregations, "it was more often reported . . . that the church failed to be an environment that demonstrated nurture and care for [them]."[2]

OUR DILEMMAS OF PASTORAL CARE

A major dilemma for us pastors is that we do not feel equally comfortable with the poor, the uneducated, the deeply depressed, those with delusions and hallucinations, the dying, gays and lesbians, those expressing intense anger, those who arouse sexual feelings in us, child abusers, women batterers, and others. In addition to the conscious desire to pull away from certain individuals, we often do not even realize our unconscious emotional blocks. Our words and other behaviors growing out of our anxiety, anger, disgust, pity, desire to be their savior, and so forth adversely affect the people to whom we go or to whom we respond and those to whom we do *not* go and do *not* respond, thus diminishing the effectiveness of our pastoral caring. What we do is no longer a demonstrative proclamation of the Word, but a negative and confusing message to the other person.

The source of both our dismay and our opportunity is the fact that *by definition,* pastoral care is to be offered to *all* in need with whom we come in contact or whom we might have the opportunity to serve.

George's visit with me was obviously a situation that called for pastoral care, not preaching nor education. The latter two would be not only ineffective but counterproductive because they would be forced on a situation in which they do not belong. I have already mentioned dilemmas with which I was confronted at two particular points in the conversation with George. These two dilemmas were complicated by my view at that time of pastoral care as being in situations of intense need (sickness, dying, marriage and family disruption, depression, or struggling with some inner conflict—in other words, a "problem").

George had presented himself as sincere in his faith as a Christian, and he certainly was faithful in his attendance of worship. He was a person who had gone through painful inner conflicts and struggles and the loss of a person whom he loved, his wife, but all of that seemed to have been resolved. He was a person glorying in a love like he had never known before. He had given no indication of having "present problems" for which he needed help in solving.

My asking him what had led him to tell me such very intimate details of his life in our first meeting was an attempt on my part to continue to search for the "problem." I thought that it must be there. His response was simply that he felt the need to be honest with his pastor as to who he was and to share his good news of the loving experience with his mate and their decision to commit themselves to each other for life. That was a *problem?* It would be to some pastors, but it was not a problem to him. It was simply an identifiable *need* on his part. He needed to be honest and he needed affirmation by me, his pastor. This was the beginning of the opening up of new vistas of pastoral care for me, although still a dilemma for me at that moment.

I had already affirmed him as a person of worth by trying to be empathetic, seeking to communicate my understanding of how distressing it is to part with a spouse whom you really love and how exciting and life-giving it is to find a new close friend when you have been lonely and to experience mutual love—the wonderful power of love that leads one to commit oneself to another. But in response to his direct question, "How do you feel about me and what I've been telling you?" I didn't know what to say. Remember that this was 1967. This was the first time in my life that I had ever heard of a loving committed relationship between gay persons. I was not even aware of any individuals living as openly gay. I had had the opportunity to learn very little about what it meant for a person to be gay or lesbian. A few friends over the years had revealed to me that they were gay, but there was no extensive discussion. I had already read several books, all by psychiatrists who attempted to describe how a person became homosexual rather than heterosexual and who then went on to describe a form of psychotherapy they believed could help those who really wanted to change to do so. As a counselor I had seen several college students and several adults who were gay.

But none of this was at all helpful to me in trying to respond to George's challenge to me—waiting to see if I was going to give him a blessing or a curse. The need that George had, the reason that he wanted to talk with me, was because he was in search of a blessing on the part of a representative of the church in the name of the God he worshiped. Although at some level I understood this, the actual concept and word "blessing" did not occur to me until a long time later, not, in fact, until I started writing this chapter. As I have thought more and more about the explicit act of blessing since beginning this book, I have come to realize that it can be a powerful act of pastoral care. Of course, it may be ritualized and be a part of worship, such as in the Christian wedding ceremony or the blessing of children or some other occasion, but it does not have to be. Yet even if I had thought of "blessing" at the time in the conversation with George, would I have done it? Would it have been appropriate for me at that time as a representative of the church? Many clergy conscientiously would say no, neither then nor now, under similar circumstances.

But if you cannot give a blessing in a situation of such a loving relationship like the one George described, what *could* you say in this situation of pastoral care that would be most caring to someone like George? Could we empathize, that is, understand and communicate our understanding of his inner struggles as a gay man married to a woman whom he really loved, but who could no longer live with this secret that was a barrier between them; his sense of failure as they divorced; his loneliness; and his present lifegiving love?

Empathy does not mean *approval,* only understanding and the accurate communication of that understanding. Also remember that the understanding I'm referring to is not a global understanding of the whole person, in this case, why he is gay and why he believes he can't change, only an understanding of his experiences statement by statement as he describes them. If we cannot express empathy with all people to whom we minister, very little effective pastoral care will take place. With someone like George, after the process of empathy as described, if you cannot give a blessing, what will you do that is appropriate to his need, appropriate to the situation of pastoral care? At this point, I will leave my dilemma with you until later.

There are other dilemmas of pastoral care. I have used the expression "designated representative or representatives of the congregation or church," to define the word *pastoral*. That begins to expand the meaning of pastoral care to include others in addition to the ordained clergy. But the meaning is even broader than this. Pastoral care is in a very real sense a function of the *whole* congregation as well.[3] The church has sometimes been referred to as "the caring community." And so congregations are, in certain types of situations, such as the critical illness or death of a member or a nonmember who is a close friend or family member, a marriage, or birth of a *married* couple's child. But all of us are aware that congregations are not equally welcoming, loving, and blessing to people who are *too* different from us, to people we don't understand, to people whom we see as having violated our moral code or even our strong social customs, to those of other cultures whose language, customs, perspectives, and sometimes religion are different from ours.

Congregations are somewhat similar to clergy. That is, we all are people. We clergy are loving, caring, pastoral . . . but to *all* people, like Jesus was—to the Samaritan (foreigners), the lepers, the demoniacs of our time? Do we, clergy and congregation, welcome and support the homeless, *both* former husband and wife of a divorced couple, the young unwed mother and her child, the family in which one member has killed himself or herself, *known* gays and lesbians, the person who is in or who has just returned from a psychiatric hospital, the AIDS patient? The list could be longer. I believe that the only honest answer is that no individual clergyperson and no congregation responds equally well in its loving care and significant support of all of these. Each one of us clergy emotionally can serve some of these quite well and some not so well, if at all. In each congregation there will be members who go out of their way to contact and support some of these, but other members will not.

The pastoral dilemma is how the congregation and its minister(s) organize to respond constructively to all of those in need, who need our *agape* love (acts directed toward meeting their needs) regardless of who they are or how we feel, and regardless of what we believe about the "enormity" of the sin that may be involved. *Nothing* changes the status of *any* person as one whom God loves and therefore whom Christians (the church) are called upon to love.

So how *did* I respond to George? For a few seconds my mind was absolutely blank, then I said something like the following: "We've been together for forty-five minutes or so. You've heard how I have responded to you and you've probably been judging me all of this time in terms of our relationship with each other. You probably already have in your mind the answer to the question you've just asked me." He paused, then smiled, and replied, "Yes, I believe I do." This response of mine was not a curse, nor was it an explicit blessing. It was in a sense asking him to pronounce the blessing upon himself as a result of how he perceived me in our conversation together. However, he seemed to be relieved and then very much at ease in the next few minutes that we took to say good-bye.

You may disagree with what I said to him for one of two main reasons. First, some undoubtedly will think that I was conveying to him an approval of something you believe to be absolutely wrong, behavior that is condemned by God in Scripture. Others may have the opinion that I was being evasive, either cowardly or confused, that I should have explicitly given him the blessing that he sought and needed. To being confused and thus evasive, I confess. I did not know what I *should* do as a pastor. Inwardly I was thinking, as a follower of Jesus, how can I condemn the *quality of love* that George had described to me and the *joy and peace* that this loving relationship had brought to him? Then, however, as a *minister of the church,* am I supposed to give the church's stamp of approval on such a union? To repeat, this was the first time in my life that I had ever heard of a loving, committed relationship between two gay persons! This may be hard for you to believe in this day and age, but that's the way things were then, and that's who I was.

You have had dilemmas, too, if you have served as a pastor any length of time. A final, obvious, and ever-present one is that clergy and congregations never do equally, consistently, all of the pastoral care needed with the entire congregation and community because of limitations of time, knowledge, training, and prior experience. We do not do it equally and consistently for many reasons: because of our strengths and weaknesses as persons, how we respond *internally* to different persons and to the seemingly infinite variety of human situations, how we relate *externally* to different types of people in these different types of situations, and how who we are influences what we believe and what we believe influences who we are and therefore a variety of our relationships and behaviors. We must constantly make decisions about to whom we shall go, to whom we shall respond, what shall we do first, what can we can postpone. Decisions have to be made. Our judgments are based on how we evaluate the seriousness of a person's situation or condition: the degree of intensity, of urgency, and where that fits in the other demands on our time, including our need to pull away and rest.

The dilemmas of pastoral care!

2

WHAT IS HOMOSEXUALITY AND
HOW DOES IT COME ABOUT?

What we believe homosexuality is, what it is that leads a substantial number of people to have their primary sexual attraction toward persons of the same sex, has a significant influence on how we feel about them and what we do and don't do in pastoral care. This chapter will attempt to give a working definition and will then review some major theories of the origin of homosexuality and summarize some of the latest research that has been done in the field.

The Dallas Morning News, in one of its "Religion" sections in 1995, had a write-up of a congregation in the city that is made up primarily of lesbians and gays. The following week several letters appeared responding to the article. Here is one of them:

> In the November 4th article on gay churches, Rev. Jerry Cook states, "I think there's a spiritual awakening in the gay and lesbian community." When there is a true spiritual awakening in the gay and lesbian community, there won't be a gay and lesbian community any longer.

The assumption is clear. Gays and lesbians have *chosen* for some reason to be sexually attracted to and have sex with persons of the same sex: perversity, their choice to sin, to be disobedient to God, etc. If they were truly to give themselves in commitment to God, they would no longer have that attraction, and the direction of their attraction would be to persons of the other sex. Having this point of view has its obvious implications for pastoral care and for the life of the congregation.

The belief that erotic attraction to persons of the same sex is freely chosen is a fairly widespread and usually deep-seated opinion, whether expressed in religious or secular terms. For example, I have known men in years past when I was engaged in more and different activities than I am now (military, athletic teams, men's clubs) who didn't care in the least about God's will, yet who held just as strongly as the woman letter writer that gays and lesbians are simply evil, perverts, and sometimes less than human, and at best were to be avoided. Some of these men have actively sought out and physically attacked gays.

I know that this is strongly put, but it remains a part of reality in our society. Physical attacks on gays and, less frequently but still occurring, on lesbians continue to take place, occasionally resulting in killing them. Of course this extreme reaction is not based on an opinion about the source of their sexual orientation or on what the Bible says about it, but on extreme inner conflicts and needs of the attackers for violence, with their targets being those whom they see as radically different from themselves. Others, not given to *physical* violence, attack with words: letters to editors, sermons, speeches, personal conversations. Such ignorance in this day of the availability of fairly accurate although incomplete information is difficult to understand.

Perhaps more shocking than the statement of the lay woman who wrote the letter referred to above is the following incident. A young man graduated from a church-related university and within a few years had reached a point of recognized competence in his work as a dramatist and director. He accepted an invitation from his alma mater to return and direct a campus production. About a week before he arrived to begin rehearsals the university president heard that the young man was gay. When that was confirmed, the invitation was withdrawn and the school officially informed him that he was "unfit to represent the university because of its moral code." The president is quoted as saying: "We appreciate his tremendous talent and find it unfortunate that *his choice of lifestyle* has resulted in this situation" (emphasis mine). Choice of a lifestyle! A university president! It is amazing the high places in which ignorance can dwell. The young director summarized it quite well: "They act like I made a choice and chose this to happen. No one would choose to be treated the way gays are in [our] society."

WHAT IS MEANT BY THE WORD *HOMOSEXUAL?*

It's very important to make clear from the beginning what we're talking about. The discussion in this book does not have to do with anybody and everybody who has sex with someone of the same sex at one time or another, but with *those persons whose exclusive or primary sexual attraction in adulthood and over a long period of time is to persons of the same sex.* They did not consciously and deliberately choose this attraction. They do choose, as all of us do, their behavior. They do relatively freely choose their "lifestyle"—the way they desire to live their *whole* lives— just as heterosexual persons do. They do not choose their sexual orientation. Not only did they not choose it, many of them sought to repress it, to deny it to themselves, to fight it off. Many did this for many years, though unsuccessfully. *Choose* this? Absolutely not!

The understanding of homosexuality as a basic orientation of one's sexual being is relatively new in the history of the world, but the practice of various forms of same-sex sexual behavior has existed throughout known history. Relevant to the point of this book, such love and/or sex can be found in Greece and Rome as early as 2,500 years ago, perhaps earlier. The portrayals are in literature and art, including sculpture and paintings on vases, and a number of other artifacts. The literature makes no attempt to analyze or explain this sexual love and behavior. The attraction and behavior are merely described, often in poetic and even idealized terms.[1] Yet there was at the same time literature in both Rome and Greece that opposed and condemned the practice of pederasty—sex between an adult male and an adolescent or even the immediately pre-pubertal boy—which seemed to be the predominant theme of the writings that idealized the practice.[2] The myth is that homosexual love was widespread and widely approved and that such love was the source of all that was good. In fact, Karlen, a historian, states that "we must remember that we know very little about the Greeks' sexual attitudes and behavior except through the writings of a tiny leisured upper class."[3] Karlen's statement would be equally applicable to Rome.

Another influence on the Western world were two references in the Old Testament to sexual practice between males. The two references (Leviticus 18:22 and 20:13) are found in the Holiness Code and are in response to the practice of temple prostitution and sexual orgies, both of which included same-sex behavior and were a part of the religious practices of peoples who worshiped gods other than Yahweh. The entire Holiness Code (Leviticus 17–26) was arranged in its approximate present form about six hundred B.C., but it was comprised of practices and laws that had originated long before that.[4] This, and the New Testament references, will be discussed in detail in the next chapter.

During the many centuries following the establishment of churches throughout the Mediterranean world, even when government and church began to oppose such behavior, there was no conceptualizing of such a human condition as "homosexuality," and people who did these acts were not thought of as "homosexuals."

Such a sexual orientation might in fact have been known to a number of people, especially as persons realized that they were simply not sexually attracted to someone of the other sex, but *were* to someone of the same sex, but there was no codification of those internal experiences. In fact, there was no formalizing or naming of such human experience until 1869. At that time a Hungarian physician, writing in German, published an open letter pleading for more humane treatment for those whom he termed "homosexual"—for "male or female individuals" who "from birth," have a primary erotic attraction to those of their own sex.[5] The words "homosexual" and "homosexuality" appeared in English for the first time in 1892, the statement being, "There is an inborn bias toward homosexuality."[6] The concept of a primary sexual orientation was about to become a part of our thought and language.

Those of us who are of heterosexual orientation find our sexual desires to be a natural orientation for ourselves. We didn't do anything in particular that we are aware of to get this way. We certainly did not grow up neuter and somewhere along the line choose to be heterosexual. Homosexuality is also a sexual orientation. Gays and lesbians did not grow up neuter or heterosexual and then somewhere along in their teens or early adulthood or later *choose* to be primarily attracted to persons of the same sex. The evidence for this point of view is first of all the testimony of gay and lesbian people themselves, and second, a growing body of data from scientific research.

Almost all the gay persons I have read about, heard about, heard speak to a group, and talked with personally, including those in counseling with me, have told similar stories. Most, though not all of them, have spoken of somehow feeling when they were children that they were different from most other children of the same sex, citing that experience as evidence that the "homosexuality" had begun at the beginning of their lives. For a long time I remained somewhat skeptical about such memories, believing that they were influenced by the persons' present experiences in adolescence or adulthood. I believe that it's almost inevitable that there is some of that involved. Nevertheless, I heard this consistently over the years, and sometimes had it confirmed by his or her older family members that this particular person was in fact somewhat different from same-sex peers. These reports, coupled with the results of my search of scientific journals, which suggested hereditary and/or prenatal hormonal experiences, have convinced me that we are talking about a sexual orientation of at least most lesbians and gays that dates from conception, in utero, and/or very early life experiences.

It is important to remember that almost all gays and lesbians have grown up with heterosexual parents and are all thoroughly surrounded by and immersed in a heterosexual society. Being heterosexual, dating persons of the other sex, marrying, and having children are the almost universal unspoken expectations. This is reinforced by the various forms of advertising, film, TV commercials and programs, and so forth that trumpet that expectation. (Several exceptions to this statement have begun to appear.) All of this places unbelievable stress on people who through no choice of their own begin at some point in their lives, from prepuberty on into adulthood, to experience erotic attraction to persons of the same sex.

Therefore, most persons begin unthinkingly to "date" in the heterosexual sense of the word, or they push themselves to "date" so that they won't appear to be different, so maybe the "other feelings" will go away and they will be like "everyone else." Often those who are related to a religious community, even though they're not aware of the passages of the Bible that speak of same-sex acts, even though they have not heard it preached or talked about, still feel that something is wrong in them, that the feelings themselves are sinful. So they pray that the feelings may be removed or transformed into "normal" sexual feelings. But the prayers are not answered in the way they desire. Some begin to feel abandoned by God and become even more confused about themselves. It is rare that they talk with their parents, minister or priest, or school counselor about their experiences, their confusion, and their stress. "What would these people think of me if they heard this?" There is a fear of how these significant people would react.

Some are still in the midst of these conflicts when they reach adulthood; some have managed to repress the feelings, so there is no conscious conflict. Thus, some number of persons who are lesbian or gay marry with the hope that now they will have a "normal" life. They may have children and usually find joy in that. But something is always still troubling them. There is an inner pressure from consciously or unconsciously fighting the erotic desire for someone of the same sex, sometimes actually having such sexual experiences, with the terrible sense then of being unfaithful to one's spouse and always living in terror of being found out.[7]

Some, and I believe increasingly larger numbers, are accepting the fact that they are gay or lesbian in at least late adolescence and certainly by adulthood. They choose not to marry in the usual sense of that word, date persons of the same sex, have most of their social activities with same sex, develop a particular relationship to the point of love, like George (in chapter 1) told me about, and commit themselves to one another for life.

The erotic feelings for someone of the same sex are not freely chosen. But once becoming aware of the feelings, those who have them can choose how they're going to handle their feelings, including how they feel about themselves, how they act, and what their relationships will be like, just as heterosexuals can. But few can do all of this successfully alone. Often they are still in their early to mid-adolescence. Often they feel very much alone.

Yet there is more to be said about what it means to be homosexual (gay or lesbian). Up to this point, I have been saying that we human beings are either this or that: heterosexual or homosexual. That is very neat. But it really doesn't do full justice to the complexity of human beings and the reality of a number of people. Realizing that I am about to confuse this simple dichotomy, I am forced to go on to say that the definition of what it means to be, or to say that someone is gay or lesbian, is far more complex than most of us usually realize. In reading a number of different authors, I have come to see that the personal and professional experience and the perspective of these writers vary. They speak of the interaction between one's biological sex (male or female); one's gender (one's "basic conviction of being male or female");[8] one's social sexual role; one's primary sexual orientation (which some speak of as including bisexuality); the social context in which a person lives and the way in which that society defines persons; and the differences and interactions between one's sexual orientation, fantasy, and behavior. There can be conflicts or congruity between various ones of these, and differences without conflict. Whereas the detail of some of this is new to me in the way it has been presented, I can see at least some of what the authors are talking about in my own experience of being male, my heterosexual experience, having my own conception of my male social role, having other aspects of male social role assigned to me by others, and the frequent incongruity between fantasy and behavior. I have seen this in more complex ways in lesbians and gays whom I have seen in counseling as well as in conversations with those who are personal friends.

Some authors, for example, challenge the concept of a fairly stable sexual orientation and indicate various sources of sexual attraction and behavior that are not based in sources prior to adulthood, especially in regard to women. One author spoke of lesbians "who defined themselves as lesbians through the feminist movement," as they united with one another in "reaction against patriarchal oppression."[9] In their relationships with each other they find an ease of being together, understanding, and support they have not experienced before. A number of these women develop genuine affection for one another, and some enter into sexual relationships.

Some male readers may understand this more clearly and with greater ease than I (and certainly many women will), but I also suspect that many men especially will have some difficulty. Those of us with a different perspective and with a concept of homosexuality such as that I have proposed to this point might be inclined to argue that they are not *really* lesbian, or that only those who have a prior inclination to respond to other women with sexual desire, although they might not previously have been aware of it, are the ones in the feminist groups who enter into sexual relationships with other women in the group. Difficult as it may be for some of us to grasp, it seems to me that if persons state this as their experience and then name themselves as lesbians, we need to accept that.

Joretta Marshall, a pastoral counselor and seminary professor, acknowledges that there are a number of different meanings conveyed by the word *lesbian,* so it is essential to know to what a person is referring when the word is used. She goes on to state: "In [my] book, to self-identify as a lesbian means for women to consciously articulate that their primary affectional, sexual, and emotional relationships are with other women."[10] But Marshall also goes on to say, "Not all women who are involved in intimate emotional or physical relationships with other women express their self-identity as being lesbian."[11] These are "women in lesbian relationships," but they are not "lesbian" unless they use that word to self-identify.[12]

To me, homosexual orientation does refer to a fundamental inclination to have sexual attraction for a person of the same sex, although early in their sexual awareness, under the strong influence of family and the larger society, many, though not all, may self-identify as heterosexual. However, later, as a result of other experiences, they may recognize that their primary sexual attraction is for those of the same sex. Their sexual *self*-identification changes, but I believe that this is the emergence of a sexual orientation that was already in existence. Marshall reports that numerous women have experiences of moving from attraction from one sex to another several times, depending on the person and the relationship. I do not yet fully understand this, other than the questions that her observations raise concerning the concept of a relatively stable sexual orientation. The major point is that there is an increasing awareness of diversity within and between gays, within and between lesbians, and between these two groups. The emphasis that I am attempting to make as strongly as I can is merely that we need always to be open to understanding the *individual* or *individuals* with whom we are engaged in a pastoral relationship rather than saying to ourselves: "This parishioner is lesbian; this person coming for counseling is gay; *I* know 'what' *they* are." But the knowledge needed for pastoral care comes only through careful listening to the other persons' experiences and needs.

It is of critical importance to understand that there is a primary sexual orientation that we refer to as homosexual, and that the persons usually prefer to refer to themselves as gays or lesbians (with the word *gay* sometimes including lesbian), but also that every person is unique. There is a considerable variance of experience within most individuals and always variance between individuals. It is essential to understand that by far most homosexual persons have not chosen to be gay or lesbian, some even having fought against it for many years. However, there are apparently some who, out of their own particular biological make-up and life experiences, have had at least some freedom of choice at some time in their lives about how they are going to "name" themselves and express themselves.

WHAT ARE POSSIBLE SOURCES OF HOMOSEXUALITY?

Why is it that the vast majority of people are heterosexual (regardless of the variety of other sexual experiences that they might have) and only a relatively small percentage are homosexual? Scientists are insatiably curious, and their calling is to develop means of discovering with some degree of reliability all sorts of things. Human sexuality is one of these areas of interest to numerous scientists. The results of my pursuit of whatever data I could find on this issue is, I believe, sufficiently convincing to counter the "human heresy" (that is, wrong belief about people) that homosexuality is simply a perverse free choice, or a choice of perverse people.

This heresy I believe very strongly to be a serious barrier to many people's wholehearted acceptance of Christian faith and, for many others, to growth in faith. Prejudice against lesbians and gays; inaccuracies in official church statements, by clergy and by many lay people; and the exclusion of gays and lesbians who are known as such from full acceptance by many people in the congregation and from full participation in the life of the congregation are spiritually harmful both to gays and lesbians and to the church and individual Christians. Such prejudice and exclusion clearly cut people off from seeking out a minister for pastoral caregiving, and they rob clergy of numerous significant opportunities to offer care to people.

Early Theories

You will recall that the brief references to the first uses of the word "homosexual" in German and in English make clear that the writers were referring to a condition that was "inborn" or "congenital." Within only a very few years the works of Sigmund Freud began to appear. He made reference to "homosexuality" or "inversion" in the English translation of *The Interpretation of Dreams,* published in 1900. There was no attempt on his part at that time to develop a theory as to its origin. However, in 1905 he presented in *Three Contributions to the Theory of Sex* a detailed description and analysis of inversion, a frequently used synonym for homosexuality for quite a number of years in the early part of the twentieth century. He spoke in this book of the "absolute invert," where the sex object is always masculine for the male. It is only these that he claims to be innate. Yet there are others for whom the sex of the sexual partner is a matter of indifference and yet others who are "occasionally inverted." For these last two groups, "the inversion is an *acquired* characteristic of the sexual instinct." While not denying there may be some innate physiological predisposition, he declares that "we are dealing with disturbances which are experienced by the sexual instinct during its development."[13]

That which seems to be disturbing to the sexual instinct is a fixation on the mother by a boy during his early childhood, which is then repressed by identifying with her. Freud emphasizes that "the existence of both parents plays an important role in the child's life. The disappearance of a strong father in childhood not infrequently favors the inversion."[14]

Late in his life he wrote to an American woman distressed over her son: "Homosexuality is nothing to be ashamed of, no evil, no degradation, it cannot be classified as an illness; we consider it to be a variation of the sexual function produced by certain arrest of sexual development." He goes on to say that in the great majority of instances psychoanalysis *cannot* "abolish homosexuality and make normal heterosexuality take its place."[15]

Psychological / Family Systems Theories

This early theorizing by Freud set the stage for decades of psychoanalytic and variations of psychoanalytic psychotherapy growing out of his work. It also produced a great deal of parental guilt and conflict. Other therapist/authors identified a number of different mother/child/father configurations that were believed to be productive of gay male children. Without going into any detail, here is a sampling of the supposed gay-producing family patterns:

1. A powerful mother figure who is both feared and needed and a father who is passive and ineffectual, often absent;
2. A hostile, aggressive, rejecting father with a seductive but sexually inhibited mother who needs the attention and dependence of her son for her own self-worth;
3. Both parents passive, overprotective, and afraid of aggression;
4. Seduction or erotic exploitation during childhood by an older sibling, parent, or other extended family member over a period of time.

There are at least five other patterns of family relationships that have been proposed. All of these therapists were reputable people, and there is no reason to doubt that each one of them heard a particular pattern of mother/father characteristics and family constellation from the gay people in therapy with them, nor that undoubtedly some gays had homes described by each of these theories. Yet, since they are different from one another, it is obvious that no *one* of them could be correct in the sense of describing all cases.

There are several factors to consider in evaluating all of these hypotheses. First, the material is presented to all of the therapists by people who are sufficiently troubled as to seek psychotherapy. Studies of gays and lesbians who are reasonably happy and are not in therapy do not reveal much of *any* of the theories or any combination of them.

Second, there are many people whose childhood and adolescence were spent in a family such as those described, but who are heterosexual, although they may often be troubled in some way.

Third, none of the data come out of a genuine experimental setting. There are no control groups of gays and lesbians who are not and have not been in psychotherapy in order to make direct comparisons. There are no control groups of heterosexual persons whose early life experiences were like these described in the theories in order to make comparisons. There were no independent judges evaluating the material.

Fourth, all of these reports came from persons who were remembering what their parents were like when they (the gays or lesbians) were children. A person can remember his or her *experience* of childhood, and this general *memory* then colors the specific "memories" of what the parents were like. A therapist has to listen to such memories with a critical combination of both trust and skepticism.

Finally, and I can testify to this by reports from some therapists to me and from some of my own unfortunate experiences: once we know "what to look for," there's a probability that we will continue to find it. We can unthinkingly, very subtly lead people in the direction we want them to go. Then they can "remember" what *we* believe happened. Recent studies of "childhood memory" in relationship to childhood sexual and other physical abuse have now demonstrated my point here. Some of these people were abused and they are reporting accurately, while with many others it has been clearly shown that the "memories" were in fact a quite inaccurate representation of what took place in their childhoods.

None of my criticism of any one or all of the theories concerning the development of a homosexual orientation should be understood as meaning that there is no validity whatsoever in them. The family system in which we have grown up is very powerful in shaping our self-concept, our view of men and women, and how we have learned to relate to both men and women (the fear, attraction, distrust or trust, etc.). Each one of the nine or more different parental characteristics, behaviors, and ways of relating to each other and to a particular child probably do have an *influence* on the development of many homosexual people. The various theories about the psychogenesis of homosexuality point to the likelihood of different sources and combinations of sources for homosexuality in different individuals. In addition, new fields of research have added important new considerations.

Genetic/Biological Factors

Given my own background of study and practice in the psychological area, I was at first quite skeptical about anything that would suggest a genetic or other biological origin of homosexuality. When I was assigned to a large church as Minister of Pastoral Care and Counseling, I believed that our church should know about and be involved in every aspect of the life of that city. Among other activities and associations, I visited several times an organized society of gays and lesbians who were interested in their own religious lives or at least interested in discussing religion. In listening to their presentations in the meetings and talking with them individually during the social hour, I heard for the first time in my life people saying, "I was born this way." Frankly, I didn't believe them. Where was the evidence? The same thing took place when I moved to Dallas and took groups of students to the meetings of a gay and lesbian organization, which was organized by and operated under the auspices of a church urban ministry.

I reinterpreted their statement of being "born that way" into "I've been this way as long as I can remember. I didn't choose it." Obviously I was hearing them as reading their present adult experiences and their recent memories into their very early life. I still believed that some interaction of early life experiences was the "real cause."

In the early 1980s I was on a university task force to study "homosexuality" and make an informal report to the administration. The investigation was stimulated by the formation of a gay and lesbian organization on the campus, with university officials accurately anticipating what later took place, the group's requesting official recognition by the Student Senate. I was assigned the task of doing a computer search of literature dealing with biological bases of homosexual orientation.

I began with as open a mind as possible, although my bias toward a psychological/family systems theory of the development of homosexuality was still in place. The very extensive computer search turned up relatively few scientific journal articles. Reading those journals that were available in this metropolitan area, I was not impressed with the rigor of the methodology of a number of them. None that I found attempted to replicate or to build on earlier research. No doubt my bias affected interpretations of the research reports that I read at that time. At the same time, I was being forced to consider new possibilities. Their findings to me were not convincing in themselves but were enough not to rule out the possibility of more convincing data being found in the future. Now in the mid-1990s I have found much more material, published in a larger number of highly respected scientific journals, and some studies that built upon one another.

First, there are a number of studies that have sought to discover whether there are hereditary factors involved in some people's being homosexual. One method of determining the heritability of traits is by twin studies. Geneticists have traced out particular patterns of inheritance to the point where it can be determined whether a certain trait appears by chance or whether it has a rate of occurrence that suggests that it is genetic.

In 1991 Bailey and Pillard[16] reported research on the heritability of male homosexuality. The subjects were homosexual men who were arranged in four groups: those who had (1) a monozygotic (identical; MZ) twin, (2) a dyozygotic (fraternal twin, where both of the twins were male; DZ), (3) a sibling who was not a twin, and (4) an adoptive brother. The sexual orientation of each category of sibling was determined for each of the original subjects. Results showed the following rates of concordance between the original subject and the particular sibling, that is, showing the percentage of siblings in each category who were also homosexuals: MZ twins—52%; DZ twins— 22%; adoptive brothers— 11%; non-twin biological siblings—9.2%. Comparing the rates of the MZ twins with the other groups, the researchers concluded: "pattern of rates of homosexuality by type of relative was generally consistent with substantial genetic influence, with the exception of the non-twin brothers . . . ."[17] In their discussion, the authors point out that attempts to test psychodynamic and psychosocial theories of the origin of homosexuality have thus far all been negative. They are careful to note that this does not mean that there is *no* influence, merely that no one or combination of family dynamics are *specifiable*. Thus Bailey and Pillard state that we must consider physiological causal factors and not just psychological, social, or environmental factors.[18]

Two years later the same two researchers published results of their study of women.[19] The research design was the same as that for the men. In this study of women, only three groups were used: MZ twins, DZ twins (where both of the twins were female), and adopted sisters, with all subjects having a number of older homosexual relatives. The results: 48% of MZ twin sets were homosexual or bisexual, compared with 16% of the DZ twins and only 6% of the adopted sisters. The researchers concluded that there is "evidence that female sexual orientation is at least somewhat heritable." Results from further analysis of the data support the judgment "that genes, rather than shared environmental factors, account for concordance of sexual orientation."[20]

In addition to the twin studies, there is now direct physiological genetic evidence that at least a predisposition toward homosexuality is inherited in some number of men. Hamer and his colleagues, in the context of a research project far more elaborate than my report here, selected forty pairs of homosexual brothers, together with their mothers and other siblings when available. Of the eighty gay men, most reported having sexual attraction to males by the age of ten, with the greatest increase in such sexual awareness occurring from ages eleven to eighteen.

From blood samples of all of the subjects, the researchers isolated the DNA from each participant. Then they examined the twenty-two markers that span the X chromosome, which is received *exclusively from mothers*. Thirty-three of the sibling pairs shared the same markers of a particular location of the X chromosome. Their conclusion was: "We have now produced evidence that one form of masculine homosexuality is preferentially transmitted through the maternal side and is genetically linked to chromosomal region Xg28."[21]

Other contributions to the discussion come from a direct study of the brain. LeVay tells us that the anterior hypothalamus, a small area of the lower middle part of the brain, is involved in "the regulation of sexual behavior."[22] He indicates that two particular small groups of neurons in the hypothalamus (INAH 2 and 3) are "significantly larger in men than in women." He hypothesized that INAH 2 and 3 would be large in men who were sexually oriented toward women and small in men who were sexually oriented toward men. He was able to obtain samples of brain tissue from 19 homosexual men who died of AIDS and 16 heterosexual men, six of whom died of AIDS and 10 of other causes. There was no difference in the size of the relevant region of the brain between those who had AIDS and those who did not. The results showed that there was no difference between the homosexual and heterosexual males in the size of INAH 1, 2, or 4, but that INAH 3 was twice as large in the heterosexual men. The measured difference was highly significant statistically.

The last area of physiological investigation I will mention is that of hormonal influence on the development of the child. Ellis and Ames summarize the findings of quite a number of research projects. They discovered that there were increases of hormones from several different sources functioning during the pregnancy of women who have children who became homosexual. One source they attributed to genetic differences. A second was the giving of doses of progestines. A third source was stress. An interesting finding is an illustration of how stress during pregnancy may affect the activation of certain hormones that affect later sexual preferences of the child. They discovered that a higher proportion of homosexual males were born in Germany between 1941 and 1946, that is, during the massive bombings and then the advancing of enemy troops, than at other times in that country.

Their conclusion is "that scientific evidence supports the view that hormonal and neurological variables, operating during gestation, are the main determinants of sexual orientation."[23] From my point of view, a lay person as far as their field of investigation is concerned, theirs seems like a very strong statement. Certainly the evidence of the hormonal influence is impressive, but I would be more inclined to say at this stage of research that the data are "*strongly suggestive* of *a* primary influence," rather than "the *main* determinants."

They do go on to indicate that they do not deny the involvement of experiential and social environmental factors, but emphasize that these must be very strong experiences if they are to overcome earlier established dispositions toward either heterosexuality or homosexuality. They state that although erotic attraction is activated in adolescence, the hormonal orientation may not be entirely stabilized until early adulthood. To me that observation might explain why a teenager might feel and behave as heterosexual, but with the passing of a few years undergo the struggle that has been observed with a number of older teenagers and young adults as they begin to have erotic attraction to the same sex and finally accept that they are gay or lesbian.

I would like to mention a final study, which to me makes several points. It reinforces the probability of genetic, brain structure, and/or hormonal factors as an influence in the development of a homosexual orientation, the exact nature of such influence being yet unknown. Second, it diminishes the proposals that relationships with parents are *determinative* of sexual orientation in adult life, while acknowledging that there can be varying aspects of family constellations that have their influence. Third, it also refutes the commonly held view that gay and lesbian parents are highly likely to influence a child to be gay or lesbian.

I refer to Golombok and Tasker's longitudinal study of 27 lesbian mothers and their 39 children, with a control group of the same numbers of heterosexual mothers and their children.[24] All possible variables were controlled as much as possible. In both groups the children were raised without the children's fathers being in the home.

The children and the mothers were interviewed extensively in 1976 and 1977 when the children were an average age of 9.5 years. They were all interviewed again in 1992 when the children were an average age of 23.5. Seventy of the total seventy-eight original children participated in this latter interview. The interviews elicited all possible details of their family relationships and their sex lives and behavior, including any expressions on the part of the mothers of a preference for the child's sexual orientation and the mothers' attitude toward men. The results showed that there were no statistically significant differences in the sexual orientation of the children of the two groups of mothers. There was no difference between the two sets of children in their experience of love in the family and of their sense of well-being.

The conclusion of the study was that "the commonly held assumption that children brought up by lesbian mothers will themselves grow up lesbian or gay is not supported by the findings of this study."[25] The authors acknowledge that the greater prevalence of thinking about same-sex relationships seems to provide for some of the children a freedom to pursue them. "This may facilitate the development of a lesbian or gay orientation for some individuals. But, interestingly, the opportunity to explore same sex relationships may, for others, confirm their heterosexual identity."[26] Finally, the authors state that their findings are not inconsistent with theories of genetic and postnatal experiences in the development of heterosexuality.[27]

It is important to note that none of the studies I have reported here as well as numerous other studies of genetic, brain, and hormonal influences have made the declaration that any one of these studies or even all of them altogether *prove* that *the* source of the homosexual orientation of male and female is entirely physiologically based. The studies' authors realize that there is much to be researched in their own specific areas, and that a number of creative people are going to have to attempt to show the relationship between the various discoveries, since the researchers have come at the question in different ways. In fact, some of them have made clear that the one area of their investigation (genetic, brain, hormonal) is not independent of the others. They might all be a part of the same extremely complex process in individual persons. None of them have ruled out parental relationship influences and other social and environmental factors.

Taken together, for me, what these researchers and others have brought to light is very strongly suggestive of highly influential physiological forces that by the time of birth have predisposed a person to develop an erotic attraction to someone of the same sex somewhat prior to the time of puberty or some time after that. The combination of predisposing influences and their relative strengths may be different (if not unique) for every individual. It also needs to be emphasized that to predispose is not at all the same meaning as to determine. But, as one of the research articles has stated, it would take a very strong family system and other social influences to counter the predisposition toward either heterosexual or homosexual.[28]

One psychiatrist with whom I talked about these studies and who had read numerous other ones that I had not, stated that the evidence is "overwhelming" that homosexual orientation is physiologically based and is set at the time of conception or in other ways before birth. Another psychiatrist with whom I talked about this same subject confirmed the physiological involvement that these studies suggest, but went on to stress that family influences are necessary in shaping ultimate adult feelings and behavior. Either way, the point is that none of the studies or the statements of the psychiatrists allows merely a free choice about one's erotic feelings for persons of the same sex.

A Reasonable Hypothesis

Numerous researchers, male and female, in different settings and in different countries have produced results showing a number of genetic and other biological influences in gays that differ from heterosexual men. Some theories have been proposed concerning possible differences in certain parts of the brain between lesbians and heterosexual women, but at the time of this writing, such research with women is lagging behind that with men. None of these researchers have proposed that their results alone *prove* that homosexuality is *caused by* what they have discovered. All are convinced, though, that some type of genetic and other biological factors are significantly involved in some way, at least for a large number of gays and lesbians. Remember, most of the research articles I have read have not ruled out certain familial and social influences. There is a need for a comprehensive theory that is flexible enough to allow for the physiological, the environmental, and individual differences.

The genetic and biological studies will continue to take place, and perhaps over the years the accumulation of results might allow scientists to piece together the various findings into a comprehensive physiological theory. In addition, there is a need to continue to look at different forces within the family and a person's larger social environment, taken together.

An article by Byne and Parsons summarizes the scientific research up to the time of its publication (1993) and rejects the findings that genetic/physiological studies are *determinative* of homosexual orientation, a point of view each of the researchers has either explicitly stated or suggested. The primary thesis of this summary article is that the different models to date seem to assume that the individual is passive and that both the innate biological factors and the parental behavior/family interaction factors *determine* the reaction of the person. Frankly, I believe the article reads the word "determine" into the research conclusions, because I do not believe that the researchers say that. Nevertheless, Byne and Parsons go on to say that the various biological factors "do not specify sexual orientation per se, but instead bias particular personality traits and thereby influence the manner in which an individual and his or her environment interact as sexual orientation and other personality characteristics unfold developmentally."[29] Their theory, "an interactionist model," clearly does not mean that a person *decides* her or his sexual orientation, but that the person, with whatever inheritance and/or in utero influences, inevitably participates in the movement in one direction or another as a result of the tremendously large number of choices one makes every day over the years as she or he adjusts to family, peer group, and social pressures.[30]

Let me illustrate. A psychologist referred a woman to me because she was distressed about her seventeen-year-old daughter's lesbian life. The mother, Karen, was extremely disturbed and bitter about it, and literally could not even touch her daughter because she was so "filthy." Karen was also still bitter about her husband's affairs while they were married, about their divorce, about the husband's getting the other children and practically all the money and property. She moved to another state with her then seven-year-old daughter, Darla. Karen was bitter about her several consecutive relationships with men in her new location, being "ripped off financially and emotionally" by them, and still struggling in her relationship with the present one. She was bitter about having to move two times within the city in order to pay less and less rent, each meaning a change in school districts for Darla, who each time had difficulty adjusting.

During all of this time Karen complained bitterly to Darla about the ways in which she, Karen, had been abused by all of these men, how you couldn't trust them, how selfish and unloving they all were. Children, of course, are not emotionally ready for this. Karen had to work during all of this time, usually until eight or nine at night. When Darla was thirteen, Karen wanted to save money and decided not to use after-school care for her daughter, so from age thirteen on, Darla came in from school and was alone during the afternoon and evening to just about bedtime. One exception to this was one after-school activity that Darla participated in regularly during her first two years of high school. Darla did everything that a child and early adolescent could think of to gain her mother's attention and to get some kind of love from her: writing notes, drawing pictures, doing nice things around the house. But Karen was too preoccupied and too tired to show that she even noticed these.

At age fourteen Darla became very depressed and then very openly angry at her mother. A psychiatrist helped her through this time. The psychiatrist had sessions with the two of them, but Karen stopped going after only four sessions. About age sixteen Darla began to go around with a group of girls for the first time. They would go places following Darla's after-school activity and at night. The mother didn't like these other older girls at all and said so in no uncertain terms. She criticized Darla for cutting her hair like the others and beginning to wear sloppy clothes, for dropping out of her school activity (in which, by the way, she excelled), and for stopping her studying. After a period of time, Karen found love notes that one of the group had written to Darla. The mother exploded to Darla, and it all came out. The girls were lesbian, and Darla was one of them.

Now the mother dislikes her daughter so much that even the thought of hugging or touching Darla, much less kissing her, makes her nauseated. She blames Darla for this, and yet Karen is beginning to realize how much wrong she has done. Even so, after only about five sessions, Karen stopped coming for counseling because she was too busy, too tired, indicating that she just didn't like dealing with all of this anyway. Darla was willing to come only one time, and then reluctantly.

Did this teenager have any kind of biological predisposition to her becoming involved in lesbian relationships? I have no idea, except to say that it's possible. No doubt some other daughters in a similar situation would not necessarily have done so. Did Darla consciously choose at age sixteen or seventeen that she would rather be lesbian than heterosexual?

That was not her experience of it, and I don't believe that that was what she did. She did begin to be a part of a group in which she found acceptance. Now, some ten or so years later, during which time I've had no knowledge of her, is she still really lesbian, or was that just a phase in which she sought to meet her needs for feminine companionship and intimacy that she was otherwise lacking at the time? I don't know, but there is no question her needs were not met by a bitter mother whose own needs were not met, who detested yet needed men, who was never around, and who wouldn't even touch her affection-starved daughter.

Also think of the uncountable number of daily decisions that Darla made from age seven, and undoubtedly even before that. Think of the power of her need for love and companionship and conversation with her mother over those years. What is a child to do? A child does whatever she or he has to do and can find to do in order to survive and attempt to grow as a person. Did Darla *have* to become a part of that particular group of young women? No, but she had always felt unattractive and unacceptable to both boys and girls. It seems to me that we can understand that she would rather be somewhere than nowhere, receiving attention and affection from whomever she could find rather than receiving none at all. Once with them, did she have to remain with them when the relationships began to be sexual? No, but the support, acceptance, and affection shown to her within that group had to be very powerful. And, as earlier suggested, *perhaps* there was a biological bias toward responding to sexual overtures from women, but perhaps not.

We shall never know with certainty. We certainly do know that the behavior of the father and mother, though perhaps by itself not *determinative* of their daughter's sexual life at the time I saw the mother and daughter, was certainly powerfully influential and severely limited the range of choices that the daughter had as the little girl tried and tried to get her mother's attention and affection and failed.

Another situation is different in many ways. A twenty-two-year-old college woman, Ann, came to me after having called for an appointment following an initial visit by her parents. She was a very beautiful young woman and very tastefully and neatly dressed. Her parents had gone to a psychiatrist when she finally admitted to them that she was lesbian, and the psychiatrist referred them to me. The parents' distress knew no bounds, but there was no apparent anger, no fighting. They, and also her two brothers, loved her very much. The parents came only one time. Ann, however, desired so strongly a more open and affectionate relationship with her family that she decided to continue.

She reported a lifelong happy family life, many friends, many enjoyable activities. She made good grades in school, was very popular, and was elected to a number of positions of leadership. She began dating in early adolescence, liked the boys, who in turn were very attracted to her, hugged and kissed, but reported that she never felt the tingling excitement that her friends reported. She continued going out on dates during college, but within the last year she simply began to realize that she was never going to be satisfied with men as sexual partners and that she was beginning to be sexually attracted to another young woman student. The relationship developed until they got an apartment and began to live together.

In the session with the parents, they were, of course, extremely pained and were absolutely bewildered. How could this have happened? It did not fit with anything they had previously known about their cherished daughter. The family life had seemed comfortable, informal, and friendly. Where are the "parental behavior" indicators of a child's becoming homosexual? They (and Ann) talked with their minister. He was also bewildered.

It would appear in this instance that there could well be genetic and/or other biological predispositions toward erotic attraction to another woman. Was there *nothing* in the family life that might have been influential? According to the family's report there was not. The only possible thing that Ann mentioned was that although she knew that her father loved her very much, he was not very demonstrative. Could that alone "cause" lesbianism? Of course not. Might it have some influence? Maybe, and maybe along with a number of subtle aspects of family life influence us all but which we can't name. One of the researchers suggested that it is important to look for things that are *not* present in the family as well as things that *are* present.[31] There may have been early events that no one even remembers as being important to them, but might have been to a child. But I don't want to make too much of that. The appearance to me is of a physiological predisposition that developed into an open awareness only very slowly over some nine or ten years of adolescence and young adulthood, although possibly with some subtle, though strong, family system and other social influences.

Some form of an interactional hypothesis of the sources of homosexuality seems to make the most sense to me. This is a position taken by one of the most active researchers and writers in the field. He states his thesis succinctly: "The theory of gender transposition integrates findings regarding both prenatal hormonal programming of the sexual brain, and postnatal social programming."[32]

The one thing that all researchers in different scientific fields and that the great majority of psychotherapists who have worked with lesbian/gay persons agree upon is that the source or sources are such in terms of potency and sufficiently early in a person's life that a person cannot be said just to be making a choice to *be* the way he or she is, and thus cannot just make a simple decision to *be* some other way.

BISEXUALITY

The word "bisexual" refers to a person who is approximately equally erotically attracted to both sexes throughout his or her adult life, even though sexual relationships may not have been experienced with both sexes. Since that idea does not fit the usual experience of many of us, we find it difficult to conceive of and we don't know what to do with it. "Bisexuality is another conceptual loose end that has been forced into a precarious niche in an otherwise neat conceptual apparatus."[33] We are aware of teenagers of the same sex, especially younger ones, who engage in mutual masturbation, caressing, and sometimes other sexual acts as a part of their sexual experimentation in the process of finding themselves sexually. Yet some time later, most of them are clearly heterosexual. We are aware of heterosexual men and women in prisons who in their segregation and deprivation have sex with other inmates. We are aware of married men and women who have intercourse with their mates but are secretly attracted to others of the same sex and who sometimes have an extramarital same-sex affair. All of these "perform" bisexually, but as I understand it they are not those whom the word bisexual describes.

The picture is quite confused. Several researchers have discovered that a number of African-American males whose predominant sexual activity is homosexual actually think of themselves as heterosexual. Many of the married men who have homosexual affairs or are frequent participants in "quickie" and anonymous steam bath and public restroom sex with men realize that they are actually homosexual persons who married and remain married for any one or a combination of reasons. There are also such men who actually consider themselves to be heterosexual, yet who "need" the excitement and release of such furtive sexual acts.

An empirical study[34] has shown that persons who may identify themselves as gay or lesbian and have these sexual experiences, may at a later point in their lives be attracted to the other sex, be in love, marry, and live heterosexually ever after. In my thinking, these persons are not bisexual, they are heterosexual but those for whom trauma and/or other situational factors have led to the earlier self-definition. But others think of this in different ways.

However, there are also those whose adult behavior shifted from one sex to another several times over many years, including several love relationships with both sexes. This is probably what is meant by the term bisexuality, although the word is not adequately descriptive of the complex sexual feelings and relationships. One clarifying insight that came from the study was that love and sexual relationships with one's own sex might have a certain meaning for a person and love and sexual relationships with the other sex have quite another significant meaning. The study also clarified, as has already been described, that simply the ability to perform sexually with both sexes does not define bisexuality.

Although I personally don't believe that much of the case study material these authors use illustrates a definition of bisexuality as one who has erotic attraction relatively equally for both sexes throughout his or her mature adult life, the study emphasizes that the source of bisexuality seems to be in the primary social milieu in which one lives one's life, the pressures to conform to homosexuality only or heterosexuality only, or to an openness to both sexes for love and affection and sexual activity. This seems to be particularly true of women who found their lesbian identity (or the lesbian part of their identity) in the intimacy of certain women's groups. Included in that social pressure is the "naming" of a person by the others or by one's self-naming in response to primary social groups.

As I have reread the material in this section to this point, I am quite aware that it may sound confused. I believe that this communicates the reality of the many varieties of sexual life to which different people apply the word "bisexual." By my definition in the first paragraph of this section, there are very few people who in adult life would be classified as bisexual. This is in line with Wayne Dynes' conclusion: "It seems that there are few individuals in today's society who have attained a positive ideal 'gender-blindness,'" that is, choosing partners solely on the basis of personal qualities, regardless of their sex. Dynes goes on to say that even though persons may be attracted to and/or have sex with persons of the other sex, "most people fall more strongly on one side than the other," to the point that they could be properly classified as heterosexual or homosexual rather than bisexual.[35]

It is not unreasonable, I believe, to suggest that the source of bisexuality as I have defined it, as with homosexuality or heterosexuality, is some combination of genetic factors that probably affect certain structures of the brain, which in turn control or influence one's sexuality, and the interaction with in utero hormonal influences. It also seems that the primary group with which one associates, beginning with one's family but continuing with various peer groups with which one identifies, has a very strong influence in shaping one's erotic attractions and in providing opportunities for erotic relationships.

SUMMARY

The main thrust of this chapter has been to review some of the main findings of scientific research dealing with the source of homosexuality in our culture. The impact of such research at this time is to stimulate further research, to build on that which has been done, to seek to replicate studies in order to confirm or refute their findings, and to add new findings that may give rise to further theories concerning what the more precise roles of genetics and physiological development are in establishing a homosexual orientation. The results as they stand, however, combine to be strongly suggestive of physiological involvement in the production of much, if not most, homosexuality. Involvement and influence are not the same as cause. All the researchers reported here either did not rule out or specifically included early family system, other early life experience factors, and how the individual in the light of her or his own perceived needs adjusted and behaved in response to all of these influences.

The total impact, even though including the child's and early adolescent's mental and behavioral reactions, cannot allow the conclusion that a person merely *chooses* to be gay or lesbian. This is a conclusion of considerable significance in shaping our attitudes about homosexuality and homosexual persons as we pastors engage ourselves with them and members of their families. It can also shape the way we lead our congregations in the direction of being pastoral for such persons and families.

3

WHAT THE BIBLE SAYS ABOUT HOMOSEXUALITY (HOMOSEXUAL ACTS)

What we *believe* can influence how we *feel*. What we believe that the Bible really is saying about homosexual acts may influence how we feel about homosexual persons. The Bible, of course, is not the only force at work in determining our feelings. We are far too complex for that. But what we understand the Scripture to be saying on this subject may certainly play a role in shaping our feelings and thus our pastoral care to lesbians and gays and their families.

The Bible is the church's book. It's the story of a people who have the experience of being called into being by God, who initiated a covenant with them: "I will be your God and you will be my people." Both what it meant to them that Yahweh was their God and what it meant to and for them to be God's people were frequently a source of misunderstanding on the part of the Jews. But on the whole, their understanding grew over the centuries with their experiences of God's bringing them out of Egypt (grace and gratitude), by receiving their Law (worship and obedience and identity), by the Psalms (praise, hope, the source of strength, self-expression), and the major prophets (God as their savior, the demand for justice, and a revelation of love that went beyond the law). The Bible then portrays powerfully a man of that people who revealed in his obedience to God and his human expressions of divine love what God's attitude and action were toward all people, God as loving power. Jesus as the Christ did this in a clear and decisive way, a way beyond which no one could ever go in revealing God. The result of his life, death, and resurrection was an empowering of his disciples to come together into a vital faith, love, worship, and service that after a number of years came to be called the church. That story is *our* story. This is who we are as defined by the Scripture. There is described our mission and the source of whatever faith, love, and power that we have: God known in Jesus, who was the Christ, and the Holy Spirit, God present with us. The Bible is our book.

THE BIBLE AS THE WORD OF GOD

The discussion of what the Bible is, what it means to say that it is the Word of God, and the way in which we read the Scripture to gain meaning for our lives, and then applying this to an understanding of what the Bible has to say to us about homosexual acts are the areas where you who are the readers of this book are going to diverge the most from one another and from me in your opinions and feelings about what is said here. Isn't it strange that the Book we hold in common, in which we find the source of our unity as Christians, is also in the various ways that we read it the source of our differences? But it couldn't be otherwise. With our different family and church (or no church) backgrounds, our different life experiences, our different education, and our different needs and intensities of needs, how could we all read many of the passages in the Bible and agree that it not only *says* this and nothing else, but also *means* this and nothing else?

But don't we all agree that the Bible both says and means "that we should love one another" (1 John 3:11)? In dealing with this issue of our differences of opinions, John Wesley, the initiator of the Methodist movement in England in the eighteenth century, raised the question in a sermon, "Though we cannot think alike, may we not love one another?"[1] Loving one another as God loves us seems to me to require that we at least attempt always to *understand* one another. In this spirit of love and the attempt to understand, I go on in this chapter and trust that in this spirit of love you will be reading and seeking understanding, with all of us remembering that we are Christ's disciples (John 13:34-35), even when our opinions differ.

We refer to the Bible as the Word of God, and our faith tells us that it is. But after having said this, there are also differences between us as to how we would describe what that means, *how* it is the Word of God to us, realizing that in the Bible itself the expression Word of God refers to the *acts* of God. The culmination of God's acting was Jesus, who was called the Word of God (John 1:1-3; 14-16), the result of the mighty Act of God and the one through whom the acts of God were done.

So how is the Bible the *Act* of God? It is in the *reading* of the Scripture or the *hearing* of it read or the saying to ourselves verses we have memorized that the Bible as the Word of God comes alive. Then God speaks to us, acts upon us in this process. It is God's acting with us that defines the Bible as God's Word, as we read or hear or remember the words of the experiences of the Jews, Jesus, and the early church with God and with each other.

I realize that this description of how I understand the Bible as God's Word will not necessarily be accepted by everyone, nor accepted as a complete account of how the Bible is God's Word, nor phrased in ways that you would say it yourself. But perhaps most will agree that it is the Book that has been the definitive influence in shaping the life of the church and in clarifying what it means to be a Christian, and that in the reading or hearing of the Scripture or meditating on a certain verse, it is God's Word to which we need to be attentive.

All of this has been a prologue that attempts to lay out what I believe, so that many Christians can identify what it is that we hold in common in regard to the Scriptures, while moving into a discussion of the different ways in which we go about interpreting the Scripture.

WAYS OF INTERPRETING THE SCRIPTURE

We all *do* interpret the Scripture. It is necessary to discuss this topic because it is obvious that when Christians refer to the passages in the Bible that refer to "homosexuality" (actually to homosexual *acts*), they come out at different places, just as we come out at different places in regard to many issues. All of us have some principle or principles of interpreting the Bible.

"But I don't interpret the Scripture. I believe it word for word, just like it's written. It says this, and this is exactly what it means and nothing else." I have heard this so many times, beginning in my first appointment in rural east Texas and continuing on through to this day. But how is it that there are a number of Christian denominations who claim to believe the Bible literally, yet differ from each other on a number of issues? How is it that practically no Christian, including biblical literalists, pay any attention at all in terms of their own lives to passages of Scripture such as Leviticus 19:19: "You shall keep my statutes. You shall not let your cattle breed with a different kind; you shall not sow your field with two kinds of seed; nor shall there come upon you a garment of cloth made of two kinds of stuff." This just doesn't seem to matter to us.

Yet the verse immediately preceding it (19:18) states: "You shall not take vengeance or bear any grudge against the sons of your own people, but you shall love your neighbor as yourself: I am the LORD." While clearly applying to the way in which Hebrew would treat Hebrew because they are in covenant with Yahweh, and understandably difficult to follow consistently, 19:18 sounds quite valid to us as Christians, especially since these words sound so much like Jesus (Matt. 5:43-45; 22:39-40; et al.) as he is seeking to direct our attitude and behavior toward all people.

Several people, in discussion with me concerning certain commandments in the Old Testament that we easily pass off as irrelevant in the light of who we are and the society in which we live today, speak of the *old* covenant or *old* dispensation. We are now under the *new* covenant or in the age of the *new* dispensation, they say, so there are all kinds of laws that are now superseded, which means bluntly that we don't pay much attention to them. There is something about this method of interpreting the Bible that makes sense. There is a *new* law, written on our hearts, that you love one another, but it's not *really* a law. Rather, it is the loving response to the revealed grace of God in Christ. The revelation of God's love in Christ is the central event to which the early church attested in the Gospels, letters, and other writings in the New Testament. This is the power of Christian faith, by which all Scripture is to be understood and tested.

Let's look at a commandment that we do in fact take seriously as relevant for our day, one of the Ten: "Thou shalt not kill." Concise, all one syllable words, clear! It says what it means and means what it says, doesn't it? No, it doesn't. The Jews were constantly killing people in their numerous wars over the centuries. "Oh, but those were foreigners and enemies," and we discover that the meaning was that the Hebrews must not kill their own people. Yet beyond that, within their own Law, there are many people who are *supposed* to be killed. Read Leviticus 20:9-16, where there are seven, perhaps eight, different situations in which Jews are called upon to kill Jews, "a male lying with a male as with a woman" being only one of them. There are numerous such passages in the Law.

We Christians make the same "official" exceptions to this very clear commandment not to kill, which *as it is read alone* makes no exceptions. Large numbers of Bible-believing Christians go to war and kill. Other Christians disagree with that. Many Christians are not found opposing capital punishment on the basis of the Sixth Commandment, though many are. Obviously huge numbers of Christians are doing some kind of interpretation of the Bible. We *all* do it; in fact, it is absolutely necessary.

As Christians, most of us do properly read the Old Testament in the light of the New Testament. The New Testament contains that which influences our response to the Old Testament. Most would go on to say that that which the New Testament contains as determinative for our reading or hearing of the Scripture is the early church's witness to Jesus as the one who reveals in such a way as we can understand it the powerful, incomprehensible, and saving grace of God. Therefore, our awareness of the life, death, and resurrection of Jesus also shapes for us the meaning of other words in the New Testament itself.

The task for every Christian, and especially for ministers who are leaders of the congregation, who are pastors, chaplains, teachers, and pastoral counselors, and those in other positions, is to determine for ourselves and help other Christians determine for themselves what the valid bases are for understanding the meaning of the Scripture and certain passages of the Scripture in particular situations.

Up to this point in the discussion, we've been describing the historic and commonly used, valid process of letting "the Scripture interpret the Scripture." But there are still other considerations that many people take into account in seeking in the Scripture God's message for us today. One is our knowledge of the life of the people at the time a particular book or passage was written. What situation was it addressing? If it is a prohibition or condemnation, what *precisely* was it referring to? What particular customs of that day have found their way into the writings that we judge as not being binding on us today? "But if they're in the Scripture, are they not equally God's word for us at this time?" We've already spoken to that question in regard to the Old Testament. But what about the New Testament itself?

Do we take literally the instructions of Paul in 1 Corinthians 11:3-16?

Verses 5-6: "Any woman who prays or prophesies with her head unveiled dishonors her head—it is the same as if her head were shaven. For if a woman will not veil herself, then she should cut off her hair. . . ."

Verse 14: "Does not nature itself teach you that for a man to wear long hair is degrading to him . . . ?"

The question of any of us in the church today is why it makes any difference at all whether a woman's head is covered or a man has very short hair or medium length or long. There are a number of other passages like this. Does that not mean that we have read the Word of God and have determined that certain things that were mandated then were custom, limited to that time and place, mandated for a certain reason, but which are not binding to us today under changed circumstances?

Obviously we need to be careful in the determination of what was culture bound in the Scripture and what was not, what was binding and meaningful then but is not today. It is too easy for us to find ways of just slipping by passages of Scripture that do not fit our way of doing things, which would make us uncomfortable, which would make us seem to be strange in this modern day. Do these passages, though a product of that time and their situation, have nothing to say to us Christians? I believe that they do, but not as they are literally stated.

Another necessary procedure for interpreting any passage of Scripture written in our common language is to look at the exact wording in the *original* language. Blessed are the clergy who have a good working knowledge of Hebrew and Greek to support their preaching and teaching. I am unfortunately not so blessed. All of us "linguistically challenged" preachers *must* have, if we are to be faithful to our calling, a set or even more than one set of Bible commentaries. In some commentaries, the original language is also presented along with a translation and the commentator shows how certain words can be translated in different ways. English translations of the Scripture differ from one another. Who is going to know which English translation of the Scripture most clearly represents the intent of the original writer without some help from those who have spent their lives studying the original languages of the writings and the culture of that time and the way in which those words were used at that time? Sometimes in order to convey a contemporary meaning, translators themselves have rendered an interpretation rather than putting into our language the exact meaning of the Hebrew or Greek. Most times in doing so, they make clear for us that which would otherwise be obscure. But other times the word chosen may itself be misleading (that is, wrong in terms of its actual meaning to us). Or sometimes an exact translation is made that does not convey the original meaning.

For example, in 1 Corinthians 6:9 the word "homosexuals" is used in the original edition of the Revised Standard Version and in *The Living Bible*. But there is no Greek word meaning "homosexual." Rather, two Greek words are used. One means soft or weak and has been translated "effeminate" in some versions of the Bible; that is seen as a sexist stereotype by many today. The other word is actually a compound of two words that mean male or masculine and one that refers to "ones [males] who go to bed."[2] If you read this passage in a number of translations, you will see the translators struggling to render the words satisfactorily, although almost all are trying to convey what seemed to be meant by the use of these words, two males having sex with each other. Two males having sex with each other is not precisely the same thing as *being* homosexual. These acts take place often enough between heterosexual persons. Obviously the Scripture could not have had a word that means "homosexual" because, you will remember from chapter 3, the sexual orientation of homosexuality was not even known at that time.

Unfortunately, the translation of these terms by "homosexuals" in the RSV is not only misleading, but absolutely wrong. This translation means that no person who *is* homosexual will enter the kingdom of God, a statement that could not have even been conceived of in the first century and which is obviously untrue in any century. Paul was in fact talking about men (and in one instance, women) who did certain things.

At least as inaccurate and misleading is a translation in the most recently published (at this writing) version of the Bible, *The Promise: Contemporary English Version* (Thomas Nelson, 1995). This version translates the words used in 1 Corinthians as "who is a pervert or behaves like a homosexual," and 1 Timothy, "sexual perverts or who live as homosexuals." Apart from the fact that there was no word or concept of homosexual in the first century, the expressions used here feed into the ignorance and prejudice of people. We already have enough of that. Why should this Bible contribute to it? What *are* the behaviors of homosexuals? How do they live? They get up in the morning, eat breakfast, go to school or work; they make friends, visit with their families; many of them go to church, teach Sunday School, sing in the choir. When they have sex, they have it with someone of the same sex. That is the one and only difference. Why can't the translators say simply what that compound Greek word means: "men who lie (have sex) with other men."

The incorrect use of the word "homosexual" in these passages is matched by the use of the word *sodomite* to translate the same word in 1 Timothy 1:10 in the RSV. In the original texts there is no word in either Hebrew or Greek that means *sodomite,* referring to someone who engages in a homosexual act, or, as defined by the laws of numerous states and communities in the United States, even sexual acts between a man and a woman that are similar to sexual acts between homosexual males. Even the residents of Sodom are never referred to in that way. The translators chose a word with a sexual meaning, but one that has several different meanings and thus is vague in this context. It is not a direct translation of the Greek word that is used. The same could be said for the translations that use the word "pervert." It is not a direct translation. There are, in fact, quite a number of different acts of perversion mentioned in the Bible (for example, having sex with an animal). There are many others that have come into being in postbiblical times.

I turned to the New Revised Standard Version in the hope that it would be clearer as to the meaning of the Greek words. For the first of the words in 1 Corinthians 6:9, it used the term "male prostitutes," very close to the actual meaning of the word as Paul was using it. In 1 Timothy 1:10, the first word is translated "fornicators," one legitimate meaning of the word (more to be said about that later). But in both letters the second word is rendered by the pejorative and vague word "sodomite."

The last few paragraphs have sought to illustrate that as preachers and teachers of the Bible, we are obligated to God and to our parishioners and all others whom we serve to be as accurate as possible about the meaning of the original languages.

There is another special case in which the interpretation of Scripture is necessary. There is the imperative to discover within the Bible what God's word might be for many aspects of our life today for which there is no explicit reference. Christians are not set free to do anything we desire just because we can find no explicit command or guideline in the Scripture. Later in this chapter we shall be dealing with this dilemma in regard to gays and lesbians. We can look for analogous situations in the Bible, but many times they don't exist. Perhaps a prayerful, open to the Holy Spirit (the spirit of Christ) rereading of 1 Corinthians 13 might give some guidance. *Agape* love directs that we should act for the well-being of others. This love motivates us to get relevant information, think clearly and honestly, and then make our decision. In these instances, it is still apparent that equally sincere Christians make differing decisions.

There is yet another common principle of interpretation of the Scripture that is usually not taught in the Bible courses in college and the seminary. I refer to the "personal interest" or "personal involvement" principle of biblical interpretation. Let's be honest. The potential of such interpretation is always present within us. It usually has some influence on how we understand a verse or a passage of Scripture. We desire, consciously or unconsciously, to soften or dismiss passages that would make us uncomfortable or stand in the way of our doing something we want to do. Or we may have a need, usually unconscious, to use some passages as our "hair shirt," something to bother or irritate or punish us, something with which to berate ourselves or put ourselves down, to make us feel as if we're making up for some flaw or sin, yet at the same time standing in the way of our doing something more constructive. It is very important for us always to be aware of this influence upon our search for meaning in the Scripture. It calls for self-knowledge and rigorous honesty, so the passage *as such* can speak to us and not we to the passage.

In this section I have stated and illustrated a number of the ways in which we interpret the Scripture. All of these are relevant to discovering the most accurate meaning of the several passages that refer to homosexual acts.

DISCOVERING THE MEANING OF THE "HOMOSEXUAL" PASSAGES

There are several things to note about all of the passages relevant to our topic of pastoral ministry to gays and lesbians and their families.

First, throughout this chapter I have made a clear distinction between "homosexuality" or "homosexual person" and "homosexual acts." Translations of the Bible have often not made this distinction clear or have even misled us. At other times people read their own misunderstanding into the words that are used. It is extremely unfortunate that many people, including those who in this day and age ought to know better, declare that the Bible condemns homosexuals or homosexuality.

During the time of the national debate in our country on the issue of gays and lesbians in the military (1993–1994), influential senators and members of Congress and numerous state and local leaders were declaring that the Bible condemns homosexuality. In the aftermath of the uproar, when both national and local events arose related to the rights of U.S. citizens who were lesbian and gay, newspapers were filled with letters. Here is a typical one from the *Dallas Morning News* (February 19, 1995):

"I am a Christian and I am proud to be called a child of God. . . . I strongly believe that *homosexuality* is a sin, and my belief is based on the Bible. The Bible is right. . . . God, speaking through his prophets and apostles, condemns *homosexuality*" (emphasis mine).

This letter represents far too many Christians (and others) who are simply wrong. From the Bible alone, one cannot legitimately make the statement that "God . . . condemns homosexuality" or "homosexuals." In fact, the Bible speaks only of sex between same-sex persons.

If a minister believes that God condemns homosexuals and homosexuality as such, this belief cannot help adversely affecting the way in which his or her pastoral care is carried out. This is different, remember, from saying that according to the Bible, homosexual *acts* are wrong or sinful. More about this will be discussed later in this chapter.

Second, the strong emotional statements against homosexual persons and homosexual acts are in contrast with our much lesser response to other attitudes and behaviors that are condemned in the Bible, even to the point of practically ignoring some of them. Greed, gossiping, not telling the truth, drunkenness and many other behaviors, and even *attitudes* like pride, hypocrisy and others are condemned far more often than homosexual acts, references to which appear twice in the Old Testament (identical laws, except for the death penalty that one requires), plus in the story of Sodom (which we shall see shortly does not really apply); and three times in the New Testament. It seems significant that Jesus *never* spoke of it (or if he did, the disciples and writers of the Gospels thought it not important enough to record). If homosexual behavior were a real problem among the Jews, if it were a *major* violation, wouldn't Jesus have said *something* important about it? Having said all this, let's examine the passages themselves.

Old Testament

Genesis 19:1-25. Many people still point to the destruction of Sodom as proof of God's abhorrence of homosexuality or homosexual acts. The *Dallas Morning News* reported on November 10, 1993, that "a State judge [in Trenton, New Jersey], citing the biblical story of Sodom and Gomorrah as *evidence* that *homosexuality* is immoral, upheld the Boy Scouts' ban on gays" (emphasis mine).

For the most part, the story in Genesis 19 is a fairly straightforward and uncomplicated one. Two angels, disguised as men, came to warn Lot and his family, immigrants living in Sodom, of the impending doom that God *had already decided* to bring upon the city (chapter 18). Lot graciously received them, as was the universal custom. Then the men of Sodom came, and the sense of great threat was the overarching emotion for the rest of the story. "Bring the men out so we may know them."

This has usually been understood as meaning, "So we may have sex with them." Some writers have sought to deny the sexual element of the story by saying that the Hebrew word translated "know" in the story simply means: "Bring them out to us that we may get acquainted with them." Boswell, in his influential book, emphasizes this point.[3] The Hebrew word does mean that, but it can also mean "have sex with" someone.

However, as Bailey has pointed out, and other writers have repeated, the Hebrew word translated "know" in this verse is used 943 times in the Old Testament, and in 933 of them it carries our common usage of the word.[4] Yet ten times it is used in the sexual sense. So does that mean we apply a mathematical formula to the translation? The chances are 94.3 to 1 that the Hebrew word means that the men "meant no more than to 'know' who they were."[5] Is it legitimate to make translation decisions in this way? How is it that ten times it is given the meaning of "having sex with"? The decision is made not by counting numbers, but from the context in which the word is found. As Oswalt says, "context determines meaning."[6] The decision as to how a word with several different meanings is translated depends primarily upon the context, what the context requires, and the judgment of the translator. Does the context require it, or at least strongly suggest it here? You make the decision.

The men "surrounded the house and they called [Hebrew = *shouted]* to Lot."

Lot came out and "shut the door after him."

He said, "Do not act so wickedly." (What is so wicked about wanting to get acquainted with the men?)

He went on, "I have two daughters. . . . Let me bring them out to you, and *do to them as you please*" (my emphasis). (Not, "get acquainted with my daughters instead of with the visitors.")

"But they said, 'Stand back!' . . . Then they pressed hard against the man Lot, and drew near to break the door."

Were the men seeking sex, or did they just want to get acquainted? Lot seemed to think that it was the former. A contemporary translation and commentary by Jewish Hebrew scholars translate the word for "know" here with "that we may be intimate with them." "Be intimate" is intended to refer to "sex," but it is not nearly a strong enough word. Their commentary states that they wanted the strangers "for homosexual or other deviant practices."[7]

Yet, after having said all of this in order to respond to those writers who would want to present a sexually innocent view of the men of Sodom by means of a rather specious argument, we need to go further and ask yet another question. Is *desiring* homosexual relationships the great sin for which Sodom was destroyed? Was their desire *proof* that homosexual acts are an "abomination"? The men desired to do it, they asked for the chance to do it, but they didn't *actually* do it, though not through any sudden awakening of virtue of their own. I suspect that not many of us would want to be destroyed on the basis of our *desires* alone.

So what was the sin? They actually made the attempt to take hold of the strangers for whatever purposes, *and* their behavior was a violation of the hospitality code.[8] In the first place, the hospitality code required that they care for strangers and visitors, and the men's obviously aggressive speech and threatening behavior was a gross violation. Second, had they succeeded in their attempt to break down the door (which they did not and could not, since the angels prevented it) and take the "men," it would have been *forcible* sex, that is, *rape*. The desire and intended action of the men of Sodom was rape, and gang rape at that. Whether homosexual or heterosexual, rape is rape and is to be strongly condemned. (In a passage in Judges 19:22-27, there is a very similar story, except that the owner of the house puts his concubine out for the men "who knew her, and abused her all night long." "Knew" meant sex with violence.)

It is significant that in later Old Testament passages and those in the New Testament as well that refer to Sodom, this event involving Lot and his angelic guests and the men of Sodom's attempt to rape them is *never* mentioned. A sexual behavior is specified in only one of the three references of Jeremiah that list any of the behaviors of the men of Sodom (23:14), and the behavior mentioned is *adultery*.

Ezekiel 16:49-50 states, "Behold, this was the guilt of your sister Sodom: she and her daughters had pride, surfeit of food, and prosperous ease, but did not aid the poor and needy. They were haughty, and did abominable things before me." "Abominable things" might possibly have referred to the Genesis story, but you'd think that if that event was meant it would have been explicitly referred to. In the book of Leviticus there are a number of nonsexual "abominable" things that are prohibited.

The rest of the references to Sodom in the Old Testament and in Matthew 11:23-24 use it (and Gomorrah) as synonymous either for wickedness in general or destruction and desolation.

In Matthew 10:11-15 and the parallel in Luke 10:10-12, the judgment on Sodom and Gomorrah is stated as the threat against those houses and villages that do not receive the disciples with the hospitality that is so clearly required in the Law.

Jude 7 says, "Sodom and Gomorrah . . . which likewise acted immorally and indulged in unnatural lust. . . ." The Greek for "indulged in unnatural lust" literally means "went after strange flesh," with several commentators seeing no specific reference to homosexual acts in this, but rather their desiring, unbeknown to themselves, angels instead of men.[9] I am not strongly persuaded by this interpretation, although it could be correct, but it could be referring merely to the whole terrible scene when the men of Sodom wanted what they saw, two men, and were trying to break into the house in order to rape them. Rape is most certainly an unnatural lust.

The reference to Sodom and Gomorrah in 2 Peter 2:10 mentions one illustration of wickedness, though not the only one, "and especially those who indulge in the lust of defiling passion and despise authority." The attempt to read the "lust of defiling passion" as referring to homosexual acts alone would be reading too much into those words. There are numerous lusts "of defiling passion."

Hays concludes, "The gang-rape scenario exemplifies the wickedness of the city, but there is nothing in the passage pertinent to the judgment about the morality of consensual homosexual intercourse."[10]

Leviticus 18:22; 20:13. These two passages state clearly that a man should not lie "with a male as with a woman." It is an "abomination." Leviticus 20:13 also states that "they shall be put to death." These statements are among the large number of different rules by which the Hebrews were bound and which are found in the Holiness Code (Lev. 17:1–26:46).

Bamberger, a rabbi and Hebrew scholar, makes clear that Israel distinguished herself from her neighbors by distinguishing Yahweh from all of the other gods. A part of the difference was the sexual nature of the other gods, both male and female. Male and female prostitutes in the temples served the purpose of the worship of the sexual union between these gods. For the Jews, Yahweh was not sexual, but rather was the Creator and thus the source of human sexuality.[11] "God's purpose is achieved by responsible use of this gift, not by mindless surrender to sensuality. The sexual impulse is not to be repressed, but it is to be controlled."[12]

Bamberger goes on to mention a number of the practices of other tribes and nations, including religious practices, and indicates how the Torah explicitly shapes Jewish practice in order to contrast sharply with these other people with their false gods. He points our attention to Leviticus 18:1-3, 24-30 as the basis of the rejection of the practices spoken of in that particular chapter. "The Land of Israel is literally the Holy Land and its sanctity would be defiled by the actions forbidden in this section."[13] In other words, "Do not do these things *because* other people with their false gods do them, and your God is Yahweh." The whole purpose of the Holiness Code is to make an absolute distinction between the Israelites and all other people. "If *they* do it, *we* don't." It is the way of affirming Yahweh. Within these chapters are ways of worshiping God, caring for one another, and being "ritually clean." All of these are what is meant by holiness, *without any other distinctions between the laws themselves,* except for varying punishments.

But the quandary comes when we as contemporary Christians begin to select from these many laws and instructions those which we accept as God's word to us and those we put aside as nonbinding. No Christian practices them all. And I've never known any Christian who rejects them all. It would do all Christians good to read all the way through the Holiness Code just to see all that is there.

Leviticus 19:18 was mentioned earlier as sounding very much like Jesus. It "fits" with Christian love. But what about Leviticus 21:10, "The priest who is chief among his brethren . . . shall not let the hair of his head hang loose, nor rend his clothes"? In the midst of all of this are the two statements that a man shall not have sex with another man. Throughout this entire Holiness Code we move from one verse to another to another, some of which we can see as having importance for us and numerous others that we dismiss as not relevant. The difficulty is in determining the principle that makes a statement meaningful to us and binding on us.

Oswalt handles this issue by indicating that there are three types of material in the Holiness Code: "Instructions concerning civil life, . . . religious ceremony, and . . . moral life."[14] The last of these he compares with the Ten Commandments. Although the first two represent *principles* that are still valid, their specific behaviors are not valid; they are "temporary."[15] But the moral laws are still binding just as they are stated. "There are no qualifiers and no conditions."[16] But how does one at times distinguish between behaviors that sound as if they *might* be moral laws and those that *actually* are? Oswalt's distinguishing principle is whether there is a death penalty attached or not.[17] Yet there seems to be no evidence internal to the Torah itself that would make the death penalty a criterion for distinguishing the moral law. What Oswalt has done, in fact, is to note that there are a number of injunctions that we in our day would judge to be aspects of moral life and that in these chapters require the death penalty, and then simply make his own decision to declare that if there is a death penalty, therefore it is a moral law, and if there is no death penalty, it is one of the other two. That, in fact, is a form of interpreting the Scripture, using *one's own judgment* as to the validity of the criteria for such interpretation.

We need to ask, "What was the 'man lying with a man' behavior that the Jews knew of?" Leviticus 18:1-5 makes clear that the purpose of the entire Holiness Code was to distinguish Yahweh and the people of the covenant from other gods and peoples. Homosexual practice was a part of the worship of other gods (and also a way of making money for their temples).[18] So men having sex with men was obviously an abomination to the Jews.

The male homosexual practice that was known to the Hebrews was prostitution and/or other male-with-male sexual activity as a part of the worship of other gods. As a matter of fact, the English word "sodomite" was used in the King James Version of the Old Testament not to refer to a Jew who was engaged in homosexual activity, but to translate the Hebrew expression that meant "temple prostitute." In the RSV the Hebrew word is properly translated "cult prostitute." Of course, the same type of act on the part of a male who was one of the covenant people of Yahweh would be forbidden.

Can the Leviticus prohibition of that act for the reasons stated be applied to the very different situation today that George described to me as his pastor, a depth of love for one another that brings new life both to him and his love partner, leading them to make a lifelong commitment to one another? Personally, I believe not, no more than most of us obey or support absolute obedience to the commandment, "You shall not kill" in all circumstances today; no more than most of us take seriously for our lives most of the prohibitions and demands found in the Holiness Code.

Our task as leaders of the congregation, in preaching and teaching and pastoral care, is to assist people to respond to the Spirit of God as God is revealed in Jesus the Christ. In such revelation we find our interpretive principles for determining what in the Torah is still binding upon us as the New Israel and what is not. It is obvious that we often come out at different points, but our continued responsibility is to interpret the Scripture in the light of a close study of the text and then determine in the spirit of Christ its relevant application to our present situation.

New Testament

There are only three texts in the New Testament, all in the letters, that mention homosexual acts. The Gospels are totally silent on the matter. Each one of the three is in the context of a list of "wrongdoings" that are not to be a part of the life of any follower of Christ. None of the lists is intended to be a complete catalog of all behaviors that are not pleasing to God. I think that this is rather evident. They are merely intended to present a few representative illustrations of a more extensive range of human possibilities. Also it is to be noted that no one of the behaviors is emphasized as being worse than any of the others, which ought to be a corrective message to numerous contemporary preachers and lay people who become so incensed about homosexuality and talk about it so frequently while exhibiting a relative neglect of other behaviors in these lists and usually the complete omission of some. To illustrate, homosexual acts are mentioned *only* these three times in the entire New Testament. By contrast, some of the other behaviors mentioned in the Revised Standard Version of the New Testament are: adultery—15 times; deceit —12 times; slander and greed—11 times; drunkenness—10 times; envy—9 times, and so on. This brief statistical analysis, how-ever, is not meant to claim that adultery is five times worse than homosexual acts, deceit four times worse, etc. Rather it is to say that the lists in which homosexual acts are located are merely representative without distinguishing at all between the seriousness of the acts in a given list.

First Corinthians 6:9-10. This is chronologically the earliest of the three references. The two critical words for our consideration are the Greek words *malakos* (soft or weak) and *arsenokoites* (a compound word made up of words that mean "male" and "one who goes to bed"). Scroggs,[19] whose line of thinking I shall be following in this discussion of 1 Corinthians 6:9-10, points out that listings of vices were common in Greco-Roman writings, including those of Hellenistic Judaism, which was Paul's own background. The reference to homosexual behavior is in only two of Paul's six lists (not including 1 Timothy). In 1 Corinthians 6:11, he confronts his readers directly by saying that some of those reading or hearing it had formerly done some of these same things. Remember that Corinth was a Greek city. Scroggs suggests that the functions of the lists were to define for the church certain behaviors that were incompatible with Christian "purity." I would also say that uppermost in Paul's mind along with purity was the *unity* of the church, as evidenced by some of the vices that were repeated in the lists: malice, slander, bitterness, clamor or dissensions, greed, boasting, envy, gossip, strife, etc., not too often the subjects of strenuous condemnation in contemporary preaching. Unity of the church and the Christians' responsibility to one another are the theme of this letter, in which he discusses a number of the specific issues facing the Corinthian church, mostly Gentiles, likely former worshipers of other gods. Paul's purpose in the lists, along with the other discussions of their behavior, was to keep before the Corinthian church that the kingdom of God is not like that: in God's love the community of faith is pure and united.

So why would he in this one list name the "soft" males and "males who lie in bed"? What did Paul have in mind when he was stating that these were not compatible with the kingdom of God? In Scroggs' study of Greek secular texts, he discovered that the words were related to the Greek practice of pederasty, the sexual relation between an adult male and a male youth, with the older taking any one or more of several possible roles with the younger. [20] These relationships ran the gamut between "an uplifting educational process . . . to the other, sordid extreme of slave prostitution. . . ."[21] In most instances there was sexual relationship. Even in sexual relationship there were a number of variances. Some of these were voluntary romantic relationships, usually with the older being the more active sexual partner and the younger, the passive. Critical to the issue facing us in the New Testament is Scroggs' statement that as a result of his extensive research he knows *"of no suggestion in the [Greek secular] texts that homosexual relationships existed between same-age adults."*[22]

One of the forms of pederasty is what Scroggs has termed "the effeminate call-boy." This expression refers to male youth and young adults who were not slaves, but who sold themselves to older males for the older one's sexual gratification. Sometimes they would sell themselves for a period of time to one man, living in the man's house as his "mistress," usually assuming the passive role in the sexual activity.

As they grew older many of them added emphasis to the charge of effeminacy by trying to prolong their usefulness and at times by imitating the toilette of women, coiffeured and perfumed hair, rouged face, careful removal of body hair, and feminine clothes.[23]

They were seen as having lost their masculinity, and so the word *malakos,* soft or effeminate, was one of the words frequently used by the Greeks to refer to them.

If the word had been used by Paul literally, and also by translators, that is, a man who is soft or effeminate will not inherit the kingdom of God, it makes no sense at all. Obviously it refers to something else. If no one was going to understand what Paul was referring to, he would not have used this word. The Greeks in Corinth, however, would have understood. This pederastic practice continued into the first century, and references to it are found in Greek and Roman writings. This word, *malakos,* then referred to the effete male prostitute. This was not homosexuality in general, nor was it even pederasty in general. It was one specific form of pederasty, prostitution by a young male who assumed female habits and, to some extent, appearance. This young man had given up his maleness and assumed the role of a woman. This form of pederasty was widely condemned by the Greco-Roman culture itself.[24] Of course Paul would say that such a one would not enter the kingdom of God.

The word *arsenokoites* has, since the time of Paul, been understood as a homosexual act, "males lying with (having sex with) males." It was a compound of two Greek words, a compound Paul himself apparently introduced into the Greek language. Scroggs states: "As far as I have been able to determine, its earliest extant occurrence is in 1 Corinthians 6:10 [having] no prehistory in Greek literature."[25] Therefore there is no earlier Greek usage that would shed any light on its precise meaning. Another possibility, however, would be if such a combination of words could be found in another language with which Paul was familiar and from which he draws the Greek word. Such a term, in fact, can be found in the rabbinic literature. Recall that Hebrew had no word for "homosexual," so the words in the Holiness Code state literally, "With a male you shall not lie the lyings of a woman" (Scroggs' translation of Leviticus 18:22), with Leviticus 20:13 being similar, "A man who lies with a male, the lyings of a woman."[26] Rabbinic scholars in Palestinian Judaism made key words of this expression into a noun when they needed a way to speak of a man who did such acts, Hebrew words that mean "lying *of* a male" and "lying *with* a male."[27]

Paul had rabbinic training, became a rabbi, and most certainly knew these words. But he wrote in Greek, so he made an exact transliteration, *arsenokoites.* This, then, would be a clear reference to any male who has sex with another male. But we also have to remember that in their original Hebrew use, the words were undoubtedly referring to the temple prostitution and sexual orgies that were a part of the worship of other gods. If they did not have this meaning, there is no clue as to any other meaning they might have.

Was this what Paul was referring to? At the very least, it seems to me that he would not have excluded it, since that practice was still going on among certain non-Jewish people. But something else seemed to be uppermost in his mind, as we have already discussed. If *malakoi* refers to effeminate male prostitutes who will not enter the kingdom, it is logical that older male partners of this prostitute would also be excluded, the *arsenokoitai,* the active sexual partners, which immediately follows the word *malakoi.* Scroggs makes the case for this meaning of the two words, and concludes that these two words cannot be referring to homosexual acts in general in all of the forms that they might take. Female homosexual acts are certainly not included in the meaning. Only the parties in the one form of pederasty that has been described here will not enter the kingdom of God.[28]

Furnish supports this translation and interpretation: "Effeminate males" and "men who have sex with them," that is, "youthful call-boys and . . . their customers."[29]

Interestingly, Luther, in his translation of the New Testament published in 1522, used the word *Knabenschänder* to translate the word *arsenokoitai* both in 1 Corinthians and 1 Timothy. This German word means raper or ravisher of a male youth. Luther knew on the basis of his research that the Greek word was not to be used to refer to all homosexual acts, but only to one type, the pederast. So there in the early sixteenth century we find the most accurate translation of the word. In *The Interlinear Greek-English New Testament* the translator properly uses the word "pederast" in 1 Timothy, but in 1 Corinthians for some unfathomable reason translates this same Greek word with the ambiguous "sodomite."[30]

1 Timothy 1:9-10. I choose to discuss the Timothy reference before the Romans passage, although chronologically it is much later. I place the passage here in this text because it is the only other example of the use of *arsenokoitai.* The immediate context here is somewhat different from that of 1 Corinthians. The author of 1 Timothy is explaining the purpose of the Law in order to combat false doctrine by those who claim to be "teachers of the Law." He is explaining that the Law is not for those who are just, or righteous. Why do they need it? Rather, it is for "the lawless and disobedient," and then he gives numerous examples of that lawlessness in a list reminiscent of the list Paul used in 1 Corinthians and a few other places. Within the list in 1 Timothy is *arsenokoitais.*

The writer here undoubtedly knew the earlier lists and what Paul meant by this word. However, the list here is different from the others in that it lends itself to a clear organization of the behaviors, thus providing a possible different meaning for those words relevant to our discussion. There are five sets of words in verses 9-10. Within each set the behaviors referred to are related to each other. For example, in verse 9 are murderers of fathers, murderers of mothers, and "manslayers" (killers of other people). The set immediately following is interesting in that the Greek words *pornois* and *arsenokoitais* are obviously dealing with sexual behavior. In the New Testament *porne* is frequently translated by words such as unchastity, adultery, fornication, lewdness, immorality, etc. Yet it can be and is also translated prostitute or harlot. There is no reason that it cannot, and good reason that it could, have that meaning here in verse 10. *Arsenokoitais,* as we have already seen, means "men who have sex with other men." Scroggs argues that just as *malakos* had referred to the effeminate call-boy (a prostitute) and *arsenokoites* to the older active sexual partner of these boys, *pornois* (prostitute) and *arsenokoites* could have the same relationship here.

Then what about the Greek word that follows, *andrapodistais?* It literally means kidnappers or slave-dealers. At first glance it would seem to be related neither to the two previous words nor to the words that immediately follow, "liars, perjurers." The word seems neither to be sexual nor a form of lying. Scroggs explains that in the first century kidnapper and slave-dealer were essentially the same, the purpose of kidnapping being to sell the victim into slavery. He then goes on to state that the reason that attractive boys and girls, very young men and women, were kidnapped was in order to provide sex slaves for the brothels. Therefore, he says, these three words together in verse 10 could be translated, "male prostitutes, males who lie [have sex] with them, and slave-dealers [who procure them]." Scroggs concludes, "This makes coherent sense out of the three successive words and should, I believe, be considered a serious possibility."[31]

The condemnation here is not of homosexuality in general, even pederasty in general, but a specific form of pederasty. I would add that even if the intent of the author of 1 Timothy might be different from what Scroggs develops here, there almost surely would be a connection between "pornois" and "arsenokoitais." Just as in 1 Corinthians, it makes no sense to include only one of the parties in a homosexual act among the lawless and not the other. Even if *pornois* were to be translated prostitute, something to be seen as a grievous misuse of a person's body, to follow that word by the reference to the more active participant in a male homosexual act would make sense only if the prostitute were also a male. Keep in mind that this characteristically would be between an older man and a boy or male youth. So the point is still the same. It would be a form of pederastic prostitution or slave pederastic prostitution. The writer was undoubtedly not talking about homosexual acts in general, even if he knew about them, but this one particularly noxious form of it.

Romans 1:18-32. In only this one place in the Bible do we find a literal statement concerning the sexual behavior not only of male with male but of female with female. God has revealed God's own self to *all* people, even the Gentiles to whom 1:18-32 is addressed. Yet there are many who have not chosen to worship and obey this One, "and they have exchanged the glory of the immortal God for images resembling mortal man or birds or animals or reptiles"(1:23). They are idolaters, and idolatry is sin: not *a* sin, but sin itself, separation from the true God. "They [have] exchanged the truth about God for a lie and worshiped and served the creature rather than the Creator." (1:25).

As idolaters, in that condition, "God has allowed them to be ruled by their lusts, issuing in all kinds of immorality, the dishonoring of their whole being" (1:24, my paraphrase). "God allowed them to be ruled by their passions [my paraphrase]. Their women exchanged natural relations for unnatural, and the men likewise gave up natural relations with women and were consumed with passion for one another, men committing shameless acts with men and receiving in their own persons the due penalty for their error" (1:26-27).

But that's not all. Here follows a continuation of one of Paul's several lists: "they were filled with all manner of wickedness, . . . envy, . . . strife, deceit, . . . they are gossips, slanderers, . . . insolent, haughty, boastful, . . . disobedient to parents, foolish" (1:29-31). Paul has given us a list of examples of what human beings who choose not to worship the God of Abraham, Isaac, and Jacob and the God of our Lord Jesus Christ can do.

In this passage Paul is speaking definitely not of homosexual passion and behavior as a part of one's sexual orientation, but about the Gentile (idolatrous) culture as a whole: "they not only do them [this list of terrible behaviors] but approve those who practice them"(1:32).

> Rather, Paul is offering a diagnosis of the disordered human condition: he adduces the fact of widespread homosexual behavior [he was writing to the church at *Rome,* remember, not the church at Jerusalem] as evidence that human beings are indeed in rebellion against their creator.[32]

Paul follows this strong passage to the idolatrous Gentiles by addressing all people, including the Jews. "Therefore you have no excuse . . . whoever you are" (2:1). "All who have sinned without the law will also perish without the law, and all who have sinned under the law [Jews] will be judged by the law" (2:12). There are no exceptions.

As a result of sin, lusts rule our lives. One of these is sexual behavior between men and between women. This behavior has to be viewed in light of the fact that neither Paul nor anyone else at that time had any concept at all of homosexuality as a sexual orientation, a condition of being. Therefore, everyone was considered to be heterosexual, although even that term would not have occurred to them either. Their unthinking assumption was that men are sexually attracted to women and vice versa. That is universal. Why in heaven's name would any man have sex with another man or any woman with another woman? Try to get yourself into the framework of that thought. Paul has given his answer in this passage in chapter 1. Yet as we read this today, there needs to be further elaboration. A heterosexual man or woman, even in a moment of great passion, is going to be satisfied only in relationship with a person of the other sex. But when a person (remember, heterosexual) exchanges "the glory of God for images," exchanges the truth about God for a lie, and "serves the creature rather than the Creator," that is, becomes an idolater, a worshiper of other gods, that person's lust knows no bounds and is no longer satisfied with just a heterosexual relationship but runs amok to include persons of the same sex as well.[33] In addition, the person does, or is capable of doing, without restraint, all of these other things (vv. 29-31). Moral behaviors and attitudes in this list and other behaviors and attitudes as well are the results of idolatry. No one is singled out as being worse than another.

Scroggs makes some provocative observations concerning verses 26-27, the homosexual acts. First, he sees no reason that the reference to males means anything other than pederasty, which has already been discussed, since the Greek words are "a commonplace of Greco-Roman attack on pederasty," which Paul has simply repeated here to help make his point. Second, he notes "that in both Jewish and Greco-Roman discussions, that topic (female homosexual behavior) is virtually absent." Scroggs suggests that Paul included women because he desired to be inclusive, that "the false world (of idolatry) is lived in equally by women as well as men (just as there is equality between the sexes in the world of the new creation)."[34] In order to accomplish his purpose in the letter, "Paul takes a Hellenistic Jewish attack on paganism and generalizes it to the entire world, Jew as well as Gentile."[35]

Neither the early church nor Christians today can condone pederasty or forced sex in any form, whether by physical means, social pressure, or psychological manipulation. The pederasty to which the New Testament refers involved various types of coercion, inequality, degradation, and the robbing of a person, not only the youth but the adult as well, of the opportunity to grow to his or her full potential as a person of that sex.

Summary. There is no question that Paul in 1 Corinthians and the writer of 1 Timothy had in mind the practices of the Gentiles (not the Jews) when they used the Greek word that meant "males lying with males" and when Paul wrote his explicit words for men and women in Romans 1:26-27: pederasty, exploitation, coercion, prostitution, idolatry in some combination. The message of these passages is that Christians do not behave like those who are idolaters, who do not worship the living God of Jesus Christ, and who do these things. They were certainly not referring to persons of homosexual orientation, most certainly not to those who live with one another in committed relationships.

Even if the detailed elaboration by Scroggs and its affirmation by other scholars is not completely convincing to you, at the very least I would hope that it would be clear that what the passages of Scripture in this chapter are describing is not what we know today to be a sexual orientation. I would also hope that it would be clear that the Bible knows nothing of what we are increasingly aware of today with the number of gays and lesbians who live today in loving, committed relationships. If this be so, what do we do at this point? Where do we search for a Word from God?

A NEW WORD FROM THE LORD

In an earlier part of this chapter it was pointed out that there are numerous situations today for which the Bible has no explicit word because of the radical differences between that time and the present: the existence of many complex machines, the various modes of communication, technical knowledge about all sorts of matters, the pollution of the earth and its atmosphere, the complexity of society, the shrinking of the world by means of rapid transportation and communication, and how the church should respond to homosexual persons today. Since the Bible could not have spoken of these, does this mean that there are no moral or religious issues involved, that there is no way for us to know what God's concern is, what God's will for us is in regard to these? Certainly not. But how do we go about our search?

A first step in the attempt to find a word from God is to search the Scripture for the closest possible analogy that we can find. In many instances it seems as if we can find none. But such is not the case in regard to the church's response to homosexual persons today. We also need to be aware of the principle we mentioned earlier of how the Scripture itself deals with Scripture, how the Scripture interprets the Scripture. To put it more precisely, as the centuries went by in the life of the Hebrew people, what did persons in particular circumstances, receiving inspired insight from God as they felt called to speak to new situations in their common life, have to say or write? Such situations were constantly appearing, and certain very significant ones in their history elicited very meaningful responses that appear in writing as Scripture.

In the context of our consideration of a pastoral attitude toward and pastoral care with homosexual persons, Frederick Gaiser points us to Isaiah 56 and its context of perhaps one of the most shattering eras in Hebrew history prior to the birth of Jesus: the sixth century B.C.[36]

First, let's look at what was going on at that time. There were the cataclysmic events of the defeat of Judah by the Babylonians in 587 B.C.: the destruction of Jerusalem and a number of smaller towns; their Temple destroyed; many of the people, especially their leadership, carried away by their enemies to Babylon. Some had been killed in battle; many fled to other places. There was no longer a viable nation of Judah nor the external signs of a whole people. The question was raised of how they were to make sense out of their own history and traditions in the light of their present situation.

It was clearly a time of national despair. What had happened to the protective power of Yahweh? What was the meaning of their covenant, that God would make of them a great people? Out of the exiled people came a revelation of their emotional and religious condition, expressed in Psalm 137: "We wept; . . . how shall we sing the LORD's song in a strange land?" Then there came the vituperative expressions of their anger at the Babylonians and their desire for revenge.

Yet among the people there were still a few strong voices: Ezekiel, Jeremiah, Isaiah 40–55. In approximately 539 B.C., Babylon was defeated by the armies of Cyrus, and another writer was beginning his work. We find his words, the word of the Lord, in chapters 56–66. During the time the Jewish people were beginning to move back into their homeland and reconstruct their life, the writer of these chapters portrayed the vision of a new Israel, a new insight into the mind of God for the new nation, and what worship and obedience would now mean in this new day.

Because of what I see to be its importance in our consideration of pastoral care of gays and lesbians, I shall attempt a rather selective summary of Gaiser's article. The Law was God's gift to the Jews. It was the sign of their distinctiveness as a people. Now there is a word that is clearly for some who were previously excluded, and this new word portrays a new distinctiveness of God's people. Yahweh is the God of *all* people. If this be the case, then many things in the Law necessarily change. Gaiser points to Isaiah 56 as a significant illustration of "letting Scripture interpret the Scripture."

The Law says:

Deuteronomy 23:1—"He whose testicles are crushed or whose male member (penis) is cut off shall not enter the assembly of the LORD." (See also Lev. 21:16-23.)

23:3—"No Ammonite or Moabite shall enter the assembly of the LORD; even to the tenth generation none belonging to them shall enter the assembly of the LORD for ever."

But Isaiah 56:4-8 contains a new word from the Lord:

To the *eunuchs* who keep my sabbaths, who choose the things that please me and hold fast my covenant, I will give in my house and within my walls a monument and a name better than sons and daughters. [vv. 4-5] ... And the *foreigners* who join themselves to the LORD, to minister to him, to love the name of the LORD, and be his servants, ... these I will bring to my holy mountain, and make them joyful in my house of prayer; [vv. 6-7] ... for my house shall be called a house of prayer *for all peoples.* Thus says the LORD God, who gathers the outcasts of Israel, I will gather yet others to him besides those already gathered [v. 8] [my emphasis].

The "outcasts of Israel" undoubtedly refer to those Jews who had lived in Babylon, those taken from Israel, and those born and raised in a foreign country, who lived apart from the Temple, God's "holy mountain," themselves now "foreigners and outcasts" and who had not been in a position to obey the Law in its entirety. This word is spoken in order to rescue Israel from a "new legalism," those leaders in Israel who were seeking to restructure their national life by reconstituting the past rule of the Law as it had been before. The new word is that the former establishment can no longer contain God's inclusive loving power. God has now spoken to Israel of an openness to *all* people of whatever race or condition. Those who love the Lord and are God's servants are acceptable to God and are to be fully included in God's house and at God's altar.

This is a definite statement that the exclusionary parts of the law are no longer to be considered valid. Those whom they had earlier seen as outcasts, "blemished," are now to be included. There is a new vision of the people of God, those who will receive God's salvation. God is issuing the invitation to all. Yet all will not necessarily receive God's generosity. That generosity is received by those who respond to it by loving the name of the Lord, being God's ministers and servants, accepting the life of covenant people, and keeping the Sabbath (vv. 4 and 6). Keeping the Sabbath is not to be understood in a narrow legalistic way, but includes being generous to others, working to set others free (ch. 58).

This is the Word (God's own self) that is "*beyond* legalism," a Word we see afresh with new power and settling once and for all God's gracious invitation to *all* who receive him. In the time of the writing of Isaiah 56–66 it not only became possible to proclaim this new Word that went beyond the Law, it was necessary to do so. Gaiser reminds us of Isaiah's earlier declaration to Hezekiah that the king of Babylon will attempt to guarantee that there will be no more Israelite nation by taking away Hezekiah's own sons and castrating them, "and they shall be eunuchs in the palace of the king of Babylon" (Isa. 39:7). Thus there would be no royal line to take leadership.

So now comes this new proclamation, and the eunuchs are accepted. Too bad, king of Babylon! You cannot thwart the plans of God for the covenant people. Even if the male royal line of Israel is castrated, eunuchs not only will be welcomed back, but will be given "a name better than sons and daughters . . . which shall not be cut off" (56:5). They will receive this exalted status if they "hold fast to the covenant" (56:4), regardless of what the Law says. One might even say that one divine word "abrogates" another.[37]

> The situation drips with poignant irony. God (through God's law) becomes the barrier to God's deliverance (in the promise). Such a radical situation demands a radical response, which is just what we get: the overturning of the law.[38]

This is the end of my selective summary of Gaiser's article up to this point.

This new Word, presented with the authority of Yahweh, was obviously not accepted as the final word by all of the Jews at that time, since there were those who were seeking to reestablish the whole of the Law. Nor was it by those in later generations who also were interested in organizing their national life around the Law. Yet this new Word became Scripture, the Word of God.

We also need to note that this new Word of God in Isaiah 56 is clearly what Jesus chose to act out in his own life in a radical and definitive way as he engaged himself compassionately and powerfully with the "demoniacs" and others banished from the community because of their physical "blemishes" and with the woman about to be stoned to death because she had committed adultery (breaking a law that has never been abrogated by any word from God), confronting those who were to *keep* the Law by stoning her; as he used a Samaritan (a foreigner) to illustrate what it meant to love your neighbor; and who placed human need above the letter of the Law, *referring to other Scripture to support what he had done* (Matt. 12:1-8).

The early church, followers of this Jesus, lived out this "new Word," the example of Jesus, the Word in their life: the ministry to the Gentiles (foreigners) (Acts 10:11 and other chapters) and Philip's instruction of a eunuch, who was reading Isaiah 53, the invitation to him to be baptized (Acts 8:36-38). Yet this word of Isaiah 56 and of Jesus as the Christ is not always accepted in its fullness today, as many people for different reasons cannot get beyond the need for a rigidity of Law and the accompanying judging of people on the basis of the law. Even while naming the name of Jesus and speaking of the grace of God, they are blocked from the full experience of grace received by faith of which Paul speaks so eloquently (Rom. 5).

You will recall that one principle of interpretation of Scripture is what I earlier called "the personal interest" or "personal involvement principle." None of us escapes it fully. An understanding of our own needs in the interpretation of the Bible and in pastoral care was elaborated in chapter 2. We speak the name of Jesus, but often we are not remembering and allowing into our own being as a part of us what Jesus was really like when he acted as the Word of God with the foreigners, the outcasts, those who had broken the Law. Too often gays and lesbians are judged purely on the basis of their sexual orientation, with the automatic assumption that therefore they are living a life of promiscuous sex. (We do not judge heterosexual people with that same assumption, although many are sexually promiscuous.) Nothing in the behavior of Jesus or in the life of the early church as it is presented in the New Testament supports the exclusion from the community of faith persons on the basis of who they are; nothing supports unqualified condemnation by human beings.

On the basis of his study and analysis, Gaiser issues a challenge: "Can the Christian community today speak a new word regarding its acceptance (God's acceptance) of practicing homosexuals?"[39] His response grows out of the use of the close analogy between that which the Scripture states and a new situation of this day. To be sure, neither the writer of Isaiah 56–66 nor Jesus explicitly referred to those who have homosexual relationships. But neither of them were new lawgivers. Rather, they were conveyors of God's gracious Spirit. Both spoke specific words to new times. Isaiah 56–66 spoke a new word of God's acceptance as Israel was seeking to enter into a new life, and this new word said, "Not on the basis of the old law, but on the basis of God's gracious invitation to all." The new time of Jesus was God's time, the *kairos*, the transformation of the old into the new. Jesus' approach to foreigners and outcasts has already been described. In the light of this scriptural warrant, in the light of our understanding of homosexuality as a sexual orientation and not a freely chosen condition, in the light of our understanding that what the Scripture was speaking its negative word about was not what we know of homosexuality and homosexual relations today, are we not faced with a new time, a new situation, in which we need to be open to God's new word to us about gays and lesbians, those who have certainly for a long period of time been outcasts in our society?

Even if we were to answer this question affirmatively, that does not mean, of course, that we hear the new word in precisely the same ways. But at the very least I suggest that it means that which Isaiah 56 says: "to the [gays and lesbians] who keep my sabbaths [remembering that this is now no rigid law, as Jesus himself made plain, but being a symbol of all acts of service to God and God's people] [v. 4a] . . . who join themselves to the LORD [v. 6a] . . . to be his servants [v. 6c], . . . I will give them a name which shall not be cut off [v. 5b]. . . . I will make them joyful in my house of prayer; . . . for my house shall be called a house of prayer for all peoples [v. 7]."

This is not an invitation to gays and lesbians just because they *are* of homosexual orientation, but to those who have responded to God's gracious invitation with the intent to worship God and to serve God. Standards of moral behavior are the same for gays and lesbians as for heterosexual persons, including sexual behavior. It is not clear to me that with our understanding of homosexuality as a fundamental sexual orientation and our understanding of the Scripture, culminating in Isaiah 56–66 and in the life of Jesus and the life of the early church, how anyone could find fault with this declaration (although I am sure that some will). Even the most biblically conservative scholars whom I have read in my research would seem to agree with this position:

> It must be pointed out that these scriptures forbid homosexual *behavior.* Neither here nor anywhere else in scripture, are persons said to be "bad" because they feel an attraction to a person of the same sex.[40]

Another states:

> It should be carefully noted that to say that the New Testament condemns homosexual actions is not to say that it explicitly condemns homosexuality as a personal tendency. When we use the words *homosexual* and *homosexuality* in a context of condemnation, it should be understood that we are referring to homosexual behavior and not the homosexual tendencies.[41]

That God loves lesbians and gays and invites them to share in the life of God's Spirit and the community of faith is a position based on the knowledge of what the homosexual condition is and its possible sources and upon the study of Scripture as it has been presented here.

Our differences come when we begin to discuss the issue of sexual *behavior.* What is the Christian sexual behavioral norm for the gay or lesbian who responds to God's love by loving God and her or his neighbor and worships with a community of faith? Competent scholars and devout Christian people differ. Conservative writers Oswalt, Greenlee, Drakeford, and others are clear that a person with "homosexual tendencies" should, as a Christian, be sexually abstinent.[42] A far less conservative scholar in my reading of him, while concluding his analysis of the Scripture with the position that the church should support the civil rights of gays and lesbians, that they be fully active members of the church, and *even be ordained,* makes all this conditional upon their living "lives of disciplined sexual abstinence."[43]

But other competent scholars and devout Christians have come to a new position on the basis of today's new understandings about homosexuality and the biblical warrant to be open to a new word from God for new situations, based upon Isaiah 56–66, the revelation of God in the person of Jesus in his relationships with others, and the practice of the early church. Gaiser, for example, states:

> A church welcoming practicing homosexuals would not be a baptism of a cultural lifestyle, but a call to certain human beings to give themselves to

a disciplined life marked by clear boundaries. These are . . . committed, loving, and just relationships.[44]

There is an analogy in what he is saying here with the *values* placed by the New Testament on marriage between male and female. Expectations of gay couples and lesbian couples would be "fidelity, public accountability, and permanency,"[45] the same biblical requirements as those of marriage. These conclusions seem very much in line with the proclamation in Isaiah of the requirements of those eunuchs, foreigners, and outcasts who are welcomed by God.

CONCLUSION

What is it that the Bible says about homosexuality and homosexuals? It says absolutely nothing, since the people of that time did not even conceive of such sexual behavior growing out of a sexual orientation. Obviously, then, the Bible could not say anything about same-sex *relationships*, that is, sex between people who have a genuine personal relationship with each other. Not being able even to know anything about this, the Bible obviously could not say anything about loving and mutually respectful relationships between homosexual persons and certainly not anything about lifelong committed relationships of love. About all of this, the Bible is silent.

The Bible does speak of certain homosexual acts. It condemns, first, homosexual prostitution in temples and in orgies, both of which are a part of the worship of other gods, idolatry. Second, it condemns pederasty of several kinds. Third, in Romans it condemns, along with these first two, the unrestrained lust of idolatrous *heterosexual* persons, which Paul believed was the source of sex between men and between women.

Not saying anything at all about persons of homosexual orientation, the Bible certainly does not condemn those persons, nor can it legitimately be interpreted as saying anything at all about excluding them from the fellowship of the church, its worship, its Sacraments, and other activities. Isaiah 56 strongly states that all persons, of whatever background or condition, are welcome in the house of the Lord, invited to be a part of God's people, based on the same conditions: loving the Lord, desiring to serve the Lord, and doing so by aiding those in need. Jesus, the Christ, in his relationship with people confirms the message of Isaiah 56, and the early church incorporated this invitation as a part of its life.

As to whether Christian homosexual persons should abstain from sex or whether lifetime commitments of loving relationship in which that love is also given and received in sexual expression, remains a point of difference between equally sincere Christians. It is also clear that we should no more presume that a gay or lesbian person is engaged in illicit sex than we would make that same judgment for a heterosexual person who is a part of the fellowship of the church.

Finally, there is nothing in the Bible to warrant harsh judgments and condemnations of persons who are gay and lesbian simply because they are of that sexual orientation.

We can hope that our understanding of the Bible will guide us in a more compassionate and effective pastoral care of gays and lesbians and their families and lead us to be the kind of persons whom they can trust and with whom they can be open about their spiritual, emotional, and relationship needs.

4

PASTORAL CARE AND COUNSELING OF GAYS AND LESBIANS

The first reality to note about the pastoral care and counseling of gays and lesbians by parish clergy when we are *aware* that the person is gay or lesbian is that very few clergy are doing very much of it. Many lesbians and gays want God but not the church and its representatives. This is a tragic anomaly. Yet at the same time, it is understandable.

A very large church in a large city had agreed to make its facilities available to several choirs from a rather large geographical area who would be in a city-wide choir festival. The choirs were to be in concert, not participating in a worship service. Only a few days before the festival began, church officials of this particular congregation discovered that one of the choirs assigned to sing in their building was composed of gays. The official church board met on short notice and voted that that particular choir alone would not be permitted on its premises. What gay or lesbian person would ever seek God in the worship of that church? They had been told clearly that they were not wanted, that they were not "approved of." Why would any of them ever go there for Christian education; why would they ever call upon any one of the large clergy staff for spiritual guidance, for help in time of trial, to seek the way of salvation? Rosser reports in his study that among homosexually active men in New Zealand and America: "[R]eligious non-adherence (is) between two and five times greater than that estimated in the general population."[1]

Yet the second reality, which ironically accompanies the first, is that a large percentage of clergy, without even being aware of it, are *already* ministering in some significant ways to some number of lesbians and gays. In the Introduction I pointed out that in almost all congregations of any size, and in a number of small congregations, there are gays and lesbians among the membership and the worshipers. Their pastors visit them when they're in the hospital, talk with them about certain types of problematic situations, and are frequently helpful to them in a number of ways. But in regard to some of the very pressing issues of their lives, we pastors never have a clue. Many of them are single and some are married. They may be nourished by the worship, inspired and guided and educated. We must never underestimate the positive impact of our ministry to them in these ways. Our pastoral relationship with them will be more or less meaningful to them (and to heterosexual congregants as well, by the way) depending upon the degree to which Christ's love and caring for them is communicated unambiguously in our preaching, our prayers, our personal relationships, and our pastoral ministry with them.

But still, this ministry is incomplete and hindered. What if we *knew* they were gay or lesbian? Would we still be able to relate to them effectively in pastoral care? Many of them are thinking that their sexual orientation *must* remain unknown to us because they fear that the relationship might be destroyed. In fact, our ministry to them has the potential of being greatly enriched if they were to be able to make it known that they are lesbian or gay and if we as clergy and as congregations could accept them as who they really are. Of course, those who are married have even more complex issues confronting them and usually a great deal more at stake when they consider coming out to us or anyone else.

THE IMPACT OF THE PERSONHOOD OF THE PASTOR

The discussion in chapter 1 of the dilemmas of pastoral caregiving make clear that both the words and the overt behavior of Jesus in his obedience to God, thus revealing what God wants of us, do not allow us to fail to respond to or to seek out persons who need our caring ministry regardless of who they are, what their needs are, our opinions about them, whether we like them or not, or whether we are comfortable with the person or that type of person or with that sort of situation. We are called to engage ourselves with any person or persons as we attempt faithfully to represent Christ.

Frankly, I've never known a minister who would disagree with that. But we know that it's not only not easy, but in practice next to impossible. Many of us are aware of situations of pastoral care in which we usually feel anxiety and discomfort, regardless of the degree of confidence we may have in other situations. All of us have some areas in our lives, known or hidden to ourselves, that interfere with our effectiveness in pastoral care.

Impediments to the Most Effective Pastoral Care

In summary, the *one* barrier to ministering consistently and effectively with all people whose needs we become aware of is that we are human. Yet being human is also the essential and effective ingredient in meaningful pastoral care.

As infants we were totally dependent upon our parents for survival and comfort. Those were the only two issues that mattered. The consistency, reliability, and quality of our parents' performance of their jobs with us began to teach us something about the world in which we lived, the world of people. We learned to trust or mistrust, to withdraw, to resist, or to reach out and cooperate. We learned to love or simply to be dependent; we learned what it took to get the love, or at least the attention, of others: just be; always be good, as defined by the parents, sometimes meaning just being passive, quiet, not in the way; be perfect, or at least be first in all that we did. Most of us learned more about relating with some of these other creatures around us, brothers and sisters. We learned more about competition and cooperation. We learned whom and what to fear and what to do when we were afraid. We got angry and quickly learned from our parents what to do with that: cry, and later talk it out; stuff it, and give the appearance that we weren't angry; hit the one who was the stimulator of the anger. We learned what more and more mature affection was, or we learned very little about it. We learned some systems of beliefs about the way the world and the people in it operated, our degree of basic optimism or pessimism, and how we need to behave to get along. We learned how to change situations in which we found ourselves or we learned that we had no impact on the world about us. In addition, for some of us, various severely traumatic experiences shaped our view of ourselves and others: the loss of a parent or close sibling by death; the divorce of parents; being sexually or physically abused in other ways; seeing physical violence between our parents; and so on.

In short, we became the people we are now, still needing the two first and fundament needs, survival and comfort, although these two needs are now usually defined in somewhat more sophisticated ways. No one of us came out of exactly the same set of early life experiences as any other one person. We are all different, though many of us are quite similar. But our degree of trust or mistrust; the degree and mix of competitiveness and cooperation; the underlying persistent base experience of anxiety, anger, sadness, depression, perfectionism and compulsivity, guilt, and the level of self-worth and valuing of others; our concept of truth-telling; and the inevitable link between our sexuality and our spiritual life combine and interact in unique ways in each of us to determine how closely, warmly, easily, attentively, comfortably we relate to most other people, some other people, few other people, or in extreme instances, practically no one.

Obviously who we are as persons affects the degree to which we can fairly consistently and relatively comfortably and effectively express our caring as persons and ministerial professionals. Pastoral care, remember, is not just doing something for, to, or in the presence of others; it is a *demonstrative proclamation* of the love of God as it was so concretely, clearly, and powerfully demonstrated in Jesus the Christ. We *represent* Christ, *as the human beings we are.* But effective pastoral caring depends on our ability to establish personal relationships that are characterized and empowered by intimacy. Intimacy requires our capacity to love and trust, to be able to facilitate in others, and to receive from them the expression of their most private thoughts and feelings, no matter what the feelings are, no matter in what areas of their lives they feel most threatened. Facilitating such responses from others involves our awareness of our own feelings, of the vulnerable areas of our own lives, and our ability not to be hindered by, but use as strengths, those very vulnerable areas. It includes our openness in sharing ourselves with another person when it seems appropriate and helpful to him or her, always keeping in mind the repercussions of sharing certain secret areas of our lives.

Only this self-awareness and openness to self-disclosure allow us to listen attentively and sensitively to the *feelings* of another, to be aware that the other person has feelings even when they are not being expressed. Only this type of listening guides our ability increasingly to understand the other and to frame verbal responses that communicate that understanding. These responses then facilitate the other person's further self-exploration and self-expression.

Yet it is difficult to talk intimately, pastorally helpfully, with people we don't like, of whom we are afraid, whom we see as being very different from ourselves, who we believe are "bad" people, whose very presence somehow connects us with traumatic earlier experiences of ours, who threaten us, who turn us on sexually, who are repugnant to us, who are dying, or who are extremely and openly angry, especially if it's at us. Sometimes we are aware of our dislike, fear, or conflict or of our own sense of inability to respond well to their needs, yet much of the time we are not. We may know that we don't like a particular person and we can immediately tell ourselves it is for such-and-such a reason, but that does not necessarily mean that it is the true reason beneath our dislike. The same might be true with those in whose presence we are anxious or too quickly get angry or bored, and so on. In response to our reactions, we do or don't do a variety of things that affect our pastoral care. Committed and conscientious, with poise or anxiety or distaste or fear, we go to the home or hospital or see the person in our study and try to respond as best we can. Often though, our best in these certain instances is less than our best in other circumstances. Sometimes we are aware of that, and sometimes we're not. We all have maneuvers that are consciously or unconsciously designed to be self-protective; they inhibit the development of the effective, intimate pastoral relationship.

We are all just people, people who need to grow beyond where we are in order to become increasingly effective in all of our personal relationships, including our pastoral care and counseling, with a greater number of different kinds of people. It's quite difficult to see ourselves in some of the terms that I have just described, especially when we know that we relate well to many people and have friends, and people in the church say positive things about us.

Earlier in my life and ministry I never would have thought of myself as being one of that group of pastors whose pastoral care and counseling was made less effective because of what they had learned and had not learned in their families when they were children and teenagers. But I was there all along and didn't know it. Now I believe that probably most pastors have at least some mode of relating to others, some feeling or feelings and sets of experiences, some prejudice, that limits their pastoral care and counseling with at least some people, regardless of how effective they may be with others and in other functions of ministry. I now see my past self, and naturally the probability of some aspects of my present self, in the statement of Weiser in a book that I believe should be required reading for clergy. As a result of particular ways in which a child and young person is raised in a particular family,

> clear perceptions of reality, the ability to distinguish the boundaries of the self and those of others, ability to establish effective intimate relationships, and intellectual functioning are impeded. Of all the factors that interfere with successful ministry, personal developmental damage is perhaps the most common and the most often ignored (or, more accurately, denied).[2]

All of us would do well to spend regular periods of time reflecting upon our family relationships as we were growing up, especially, though not at all exclusively, in regard to our attitudes toward and feelings and beliefs about gays and lesbians. What did we learn at home and school (outside the classroom, of course!) and other places? Did we have any personal experiences with gays and lesbians? How did our friends feel about them? What might be influencing our responses to them now? What are our fears, our misconceptions?

Impediments to Ministry with Gays and Lesbians

In this section the focus is to be on the feelings and other reactions that some pastors have toward gays and lesbians and that would interfere with the type of pastoral relationship I have earlier attempted to describe.

Homophobia and heterosexism. The source of many experiences of discomfort is what many people today are calling homophobia, literally meaning "fear of sameness," but used more narrowly to mean "same sex." But that's not precisely what a lot of speakers and writers mean, either. Rather, the word has come to refer not only to the conscious experience of fear but to other reactions growing out of fear and sometimes from other sources: prejudice, anger, hatred, discrimination.

More recently I have also heard and read the word *heterosexism* used instead of or in addition to *homophobia*. I'll have to admit that the first time I heard the word *gay* spoken by gays and the word *homophobia* used in an address and in conversation, I inwardly flinched and felt somewhat self-protective. That, of course, was the automatic response of my heterosexism. I can say that now because I think I am aware of its meaning. Let me elaborate.

I am heterosexual; I understand it and love it.

When I was twelve or so, I discovered at least something about the meaning of some of "those words," which for several years I had been hearing the older boys using about other boys on the schoolground as we played ball. The meaning was conveyed very crudely in schoolground boys' language. I heard it, but I still couldn't comprehend it.

Now I can realize how the whole of society is organized on the basis of heterosexuality; that's just the principle of majority rule without any thought that anything else exists or should exist.

"The Lord created male and female." Right?

That's who I was, my parents were, my closest friends and their parents were, everything about me was, I thought. I had a girlfriend, and then another. And then another, et cetera. And then I married. I loved the whole thing. Everyone supported it.

Then at some age, all of us heterosexuals discover that there are males and females who love and desire others of the same sex. How can that be? We can't even comprehend it.

One young man told me that when he told his parents he was gay, one of them instantly replied, "Well, what do you want to do that for?" They were unbelieving! Their son had just told them that he was from another planet. This was totally outside the realm of their experience.

Most of us who respond as if everyone ought to be like we are aren't really bad people. We just don't get it.

It seems to be a major piece of evidence of the reality of original sin (however, we may differ in how we describe the meaning of that term) that the people who are in the majority always want to keep the people of the minority separate, apart, down underneath if possible. We see it in every country of the world that I know anything about. Their being *different* (that is, from us) is a threat to us. Isn't that weird?

This leads inevitably to discrimination, often anger and hatred, sometimes violence, with the extreme being genocide. Even in its milder forms, it is social ostracism, no desire to understand or be close, exclusiveness, and discriminatory laws even when they make no logical sense. (A number of us in the United States can remember "white" and "colored" water fountains.)

Gays and lesbians have experienced *all* of this within their own families (even to the point, when they were older teenagers or young adults, of being banished from their home, of being disinherited). They experience it within the state and nation and the world, including, God save us, the church.

This is heterosexism and often may be homophobia also. We may be "good" people in most ways; we may not be violent or cruel; we may not experience hate and some of the worst feelings, but at the core we are heterosexists. Let's face it, even lovingly we'd prefer it if "they" changed. But most of them by far not only don't change but can't change, and an increasing number don't really want to. But *we* can change; we can be saved from our homophobia and heterosexism.

And this is the point: if we're going to be Christ's servants to all those in need whose needs we become aware of (being a neighbor to our neighbor), then it is our Lord who calls *us* to change *our* attitudes and feelings and who can assist us in doing it. In fact, such change *is* called for, along with our being saved from racism, sexism (male/female), social classism, and other spiritual limitations if we're to become more fully Christian, "more like the Master." Merely being ordained or being in some other designated Christian vocation does not blot out all our transgressions, among them our deep-seated and often unconscious biases.

Interestingly, but quite understandably, once we think of it, many, if not most, teenagers and young men and women who begin to realize that their sexual attractions are primarily or exclusively to persons of the same sex, almost immediately begin to question or recoil from these experiences themselves. After all, they grew up in the same heterosexually organized society, almost always with heterosexual parents who had heterosexual expectations of their children, and if church-related, in a heterosexually-oriented church. Ironically, gays and lesbians themselves usually move into their new experience as heterosexists, too. For them, their early training as heterosexists is the source of considerable conflict, often guilt, perhaps a sense of failure, the attempt to adjust socially with this understanding of who they are sexually. This is the source of suicidal feelings and too often suicide itself, especially among teenagers.

To the degree that we are heterosexist, to that degree there will be blocks and distortions in our relationships with lesbians and gays whom we are trying to serve as pastors, and that goes for gay and lesbian pastors as well. When heterosexual clergy are being pastor/counselor to persons known to them as gay or lesbian, we "must constantly monitor our own . . . manifestation of heterosexual bias."[3] Otherwise we will probably reinforce the heterosexism that may still be a part of the personality of the gay or lesbian, thus continuing, even exacerbating, the internal conflict they are struggling to resolve. To the extent that our heterosexism is well entrenched, our unease in attempting to be effectively pastoral shows through to the other person(s) and inhibits the relationship of trust between us that is so necessary. "It is our responsibility not to pass [*our*] problem along to our clients"[4] (or parishioners).

The gay or lesbian pastor. Although lesbian and gay pastors may have a head start in dealing with their heterosexism, they do not necessarily have a head start in their pastoral counseling of gays and lesbians if they have not come out, if they are carrying the burden of their secret. Gay male pastors, more than lesbian pastors, are likely to be married and have children, and they also have a congregation. They don't want to lose any of these. They sincerely want to continue their work for God and church. Sometimes they have revealed their secret to their spouses who occasionally are willing to continue in the marriage, although more often not. Many of these men are trying to remain faithful to their wives, and some succeed. But many seek sexual gratification elsewhere, sometimes falling in love with another man, yet still living in their heterosexual family and serving their churches as faithfully as they can. Those with whom I have talked describe the burden, the strain, the constant being on guard to protect themselves, the guilt. They usually feel the need to protect their private reality even more when they are involved in the process of pastoral care, and especially pastoral counseling, with other gays and lesbians. The temptation is to let down their guard, but they dare not. So there is a serious interference with the intimacy and honesty that effective pastoral counseling requires. Many lesbian clergy are not free from this stress and strain themselves. The hindrance to effective pastoral care and counseling is always greater when the hidden part of ourselves is connected with the issues raised by the person seeking our help.

A young person (or perhaps someone who is in her or his twenties, rarely older) comes to the pastor and begins talking about having occasional fantasies involving someone of the same sex, is worried that he or she is gay, is feeling frightened about what this means, is consumed with guilt—any one or a combination of these. The gay or lesbian pastor is no longer troubled by these experiences. From this pastor's perspective it is unnecessary for the person to be so troubled. So, consciously or unconsciously, she or he begins to reassure the person that these sexual feelings can be normal; that he or she has nothing to fear; God loves her or him just as he or she is, and so forth. When this is said *prematurely,* it doesn't allow time to hear the person's story in full, the details of the inner conflicts, the awfulness of the guilt, the concerns about relationships with peers and parents. This premature reassuring way of dealing with the person does him or her a disservice and does not take the person seriously, just as much as the pastor who would cut a person off with condemnation, stating that the Bible says it's an "abomination to the Lord."

Gay and lesbian pastors, no less than heterosexual ones, may at times be sexually attracted to a parishioner. In the context of a pastoral care or counseling relationship these sexual feelings can be, although are not inevitably, a barrier to the effectiveness of pastoral functioning. What can we do to remain faithful to our calling to Christian ministry, not only in refraining from an overt sexual relationship with the person but in helping the other person as much as we possibly can? Let's not fool ourselves into thinking that we can be sexually attracted to a parishioner without its affecting our behavior with the person, even when there is no conscious communication of our feelings and no direct acting upon them, unless we have reached a high level of personal growth and skill. Gay and lesbian pastors, in their attempt to deal with their sexual attraction, also need to avoid the extreme of leaning over backwards to avoid sending any clue of their sexual orientation by consciously or unconsciously communicating a bias against the gay or lesbian parishioner. I am reminded of the United States congressman of a number of years ago who was a crusader against "homosexuality," both in his speeches and in legislation he proposed, only to have the fact discovered after a few years that he himself was gay.

So what is the lesbian or gay pastor to do in order not to contaminate and complicate the helping relationship with a gay or lesbian person when sexually attracted to that person or when he or she becomes aware of putting up an emotional protective barrier between herself or himself and the other? The very same thing that heterosexual pastors do when they're sexually aroused and/or become defensive in order not to experience their sexual feelings.

First, we can make an appointment with a competent experienced psychotherapist who can help us grow to the place in our own personal and professional lives where we know how to be aware of our feelings, how not to allow them to interfere in the helping relationship, and in fact how to use our self-awareness for the developing insight and well-being of the other person. Second, if necessary, we can refer the other person to another pastor or psychotherapist in whom we have confidence.

The heterosexual pastor. A gay or lesbian has been having pastoral conversations with us who are heterosexual. We may or may not have knowledge about the person's sexual orientation. Then as the conversations progress, the person gives clues that we may or may not have noticed, that we may or may not have interpreted correctly, and/or states to us directly that she or he is sexually attracted to us, is having sexual feelings toward us. I have known of male clergy who have either tried to cover the situation with a barrage of religious language that resulted in the person's leaving, or covered their own anxiety with anger and directly cut off the conversation.

What is the reason for this negative response? The general answer is simple and has been stated earlier: something about our past experiences and learning of myths about gays, our prejudice. But what is there realistically to fear? Without the fear, I believe that anger would not be aroused. What's the source of the insecurity? The result of these internal reactions produces behavior on our part that leads to the abandonment of the pastoral relationship and a reinforcement of the gay's own self-doubt, lack of self-worth, poor opinion of ministers, or whatever. We know absolutely that Jesus would not have reacted this way to a person in need. Even in this situation, with whatever genuine feelings we have, we need to remain pastors to them. This *is* our calling, is it not?

In all honesty, I don't know how I would have reacted in the first few years of my ministry if a gay man had expressed sexual feelings toward me. The first time that it took place was fairly late in my ministry and after having had considerable supervised experience in counseling. My initial reaction was an awareness of being unprepared to deal with this. I had a fleeting few seconds of mild anxiety but then began to respond in ways learned in my training, although this specific occasion had never arisen in supervision.

I had seen this man in his mid-twenties probably eight or nine times, approximately weekly. He had had a childhood and adolescence that had not prepared him well for life in the real world. He had come to see me originally because his religious convictions led him to be disturbed by his homosexual feelings. He had earlier said that he had never had sex with another person, male or female, and that he at sometimes had sexual feelings toward women. The conversation went approximately like the following:

Bob *(in the context of conversation concerning his sexual feelings):* I'm even beginning to have sexual feelings towards you.

David: Are you having them right at this moment?

Bob: Yes.

David: How do you feel about being sexually attracted to me?

Bob *(blushing):* I'm pretty anxious. . . . I'm embarrassed. . . . Actually I feel a little guilty about it.

David: Like there are certain people you ought not to have sexual feelings toward.

Bob: Yes, that's right. After all, you're a minister.

David: Well, my experience is that people just have sexual feelings when they have them, regardless of where or when or who the person is.

Bob: I hadn't really ever thought of that.

David: Have you had these feelings toward me before this conversation today?

Bob: Yes.

David: Do you have them all the time, or every time you see me?

Bob: No.

David: I wonder what makes the difference?

Bob *(pause):* I don't know.

David: Would you be willing to explore this with me? If you do sometimes and don't sometimes, I imagine there's a reason for that, and if we could discover the reason, we might be able to find out some other things that might be helpful to you.

Bob: OK.

We continued to try to connect the occurrences of his sexual feelings toward me with other things that were going on in his life at those times. After a while it became apparent that he had the feelings at times when he was the loneliest, which led to the connecting of his homosexual feelings towards other men also when he was the loneliest.

What had my approach accomplished? First, it alleviated his anxiety, embarrassment, and guilt, which he felt right at the time in his relationship with me and allowed us to continue to talk freely and honestly with each other. Second, talking about his feelings toward me in an increasingly unemotional and open and matter-of-fact way separated his feelings from his fantasies about me. Fantasies furnish the generating power of much of the sexual feelings that most of us have. Third, it led to the very important discovery that he had sexual feelings toward men only when he was very lonely. The first step after this was looking at the actions that he could take to avoid and/or diminish the intensity of his periods of loneliness and that led to his becoming a more socially adept and thus a basically happier person.

What I did with him is undoubtedly not the only way that a pastor could respond constructively. But these, and probably some other approaches, defused his present sexual feelings, communicated that I was not going to respond sexually, and kept us talking in a constructive pastoral relationship.

This approach is also the most helpful for a heterosexual pastor when a person of the other sex expresses sexual feelings to him or her.

Our convictions: help or hindrance? As Christians and as Christian ministers we cannot avoid having convictions, and, in fact, it is essential that we *do* have them. We wouldn't be who we are without them. And all of us have opinions and convictions about "homosexuality," "homosexuals," "homosexual" sexual behavior, and *the* biblical position (or biblical positions) on all of this. Although I may be misreading them, my experience is that gays' and lesbians' distrust of the clergy is not that they think that we believe what they do sexually is wrong (they tend to expect that), but how understanding and accepting we will be and how we will express ourselves to them if they come to us for help with something in their lives that is associated with their being lesbian or gay. In other words, I believe that the critical issue is whether those pastors who believe that "homosexuality and/or homosexual behavior" is wrong can still be compassionate, skillful, and helpful to the gay or lesbian person in spite of or along with their convictions, rather than their convictions being expressed in such a way that the persons seeking counsel will be offended, hurt, angered, and pushed away from the pastors and farther away from the church.

Earl Wilson, a psychologist who is a conservative Christian, makes a clear distinction between a person's *being* gay and the behavior, that is, sex between two men or between two women. He clearly states that he believes "the practice of homosexuality is sin."[5] Yet as a loving Christian and a sensitive and well-trained therapist, he does not allow his belief to prejudge a gay client nor to stand in the way of the best approach to counseling.

> The goals of the initial interview are always the same, regardless of the problem. I always strive for two things: (1) establish a strong relationship of trust with the counselees, and (2) to reach some agreement as to goals we will work toward . . . .[6]

It is not what we *believe* that can block a helping pastoral relationship, but how we *feel* and how our feelings shape what we say, how we say it, and our body language as well. Wilson demonstrates throughout his book procedures and relationships that have the highest probability of being helpful. There is no shrinking back, no prejudgment, no hatred, no condemnation, no fear, and no anger, all without compromising his convictions.

Larry Graham summarizes the experiences with clergy of the gays and lesbians he interviewed:

> When helpful, pastors and chaplains were reported as "good listeners," "understanding," and "accepting." They were most helpful when they understood the dynamics of coming out and the complexities of relationships in the lesbian and gay context.[7]

If we don't have such an understanding initially, and most of us don't, we can gain this understanding and the person's trust as well, by our acceptance of the person, our noncondemnatory attitude, our attentive listening, our expressions of empathy (see pp. 12–13), "hanging in there" with the person, and encouraging her or him to "hang in there" with us.

Wilson frequently reminds counselors not to be trapped by their stereotype of gays or lesbians. He puts it succinctly: "Look for the person—don't get lost in the stereotype!"[8] When we allow our stereotype to "click in" automatically, we assume that we *know* exactly who he or she *is*. Look beyond the stereotype and get to know the *person*. This is the first step in effective counseling. That's what I had been trying to do with George, whom I presented in chapter 1: responding with empathy, encouraging further detail. Nothing else. George had gone to a pastor whom he had reason to believe he could trust, even though he had no idea what that pastor thought about homosexuality. He begins in the way presented in chapter 1, getting to the point of describing his love relationship with another man. George is watching the pastor very closely. After a good deal of detail, he pauses and asks, "I wonder what you think about what I'm telling you?"

You may recall my own mental struggle in attempting to respond to George. I was trying to say something that would be helpful to him while at the same time maintaining my integrity. Now let's look at a fictional pastor who is asked the same question, "I want to know what you think about me and what I've told you." This pastor genuinely believes that homosexual acts are forbidden by the Bible and that George is getting deeper and deeper into a sinful life that is expressly condemned by God.

George, we might as well stop right here. You're bound to know that the Bible condemns what you're doing, and therefore I have to condemn it too. Your only hope is to stop what you're doing, repent, and let Christ change your life.

Authentic, but is it a helpful *pastoral* ministry at this point? Try to feel what George might feel when he has been told this by someone he thought he could trust to be helpful to him. George receives no help, only a reinforcement of what he has undoubtedly heard many times before. He turns away, hurt and sorrowful. It would seem to me that he might now be reluctant to continue to worship in this pastor's church. Thus he will be cut off, not only from the pastor, but also from the Christian community and from worship. Wilson has something to say to this fictional (?) pastor.

Many counselors, particularly those with a high view of the Scripture, believe that their job is to straighten people out. They sometimes enter the counseling session armed with the "Truth" and intent on changing their counselees, if not the whole world. They fail! It doesn't work. Differences in perception are not changed by logic.[9]

Understand, I am most certainly not suggesting that the pastor lie or pretend to be something other than what she or he really is. The pastoral issue is to understand the most helpful *pastoral* approach and *when* and *how* to express our convictions. Being called by God means being called to be as helpful as possible to every person with whom we are engaged as pastor. They will only be cut off and driven away by our compulsive need to unload our biases or even what we take to be our unbiased convictions. Our need as pastoral counselors is to find a way to continue the conversation to the point that we know what George is seeking in his taking the initiative for his conversation with us. Our need is to attempt to understand his need and *then* determine our most helpful responses.

George asks, "I wonder what you think about what I'm telling you?" Regardless of what you believe the Bible says about homosexuality (actually, homosexual *behavior*), there are numerous ways of responding that can be helpful without your having to be dishonest. We need to have words that will elicit George's further self-expression and self-exploration. To be helpful it must not be something that will terminate the conversation. He doesn't have to feel unwelcome in the congregation. If George experiences being understood, he will talk on. There is time for yet another conversation for him.

Certainly at some point in the future a discussion of what researchers say about the origin of homosexuality and of what the Bible says or does not say about it may be relevant, and is often necessary, but rarely in the first session with a person.

The Scripture can be authoritative for people in terms of its leading to change in their minds and lives when their emotional protective barriers are lowered. This takes place in a conversation with a trusted and competent person. It is well for us pastors to realize that at some times we may declare the Bible as authoritative on a particular issue as a means of our own self-protection. The pastor who relates to people in an authoritarian manner cannot compel change in persons, even when he or she asserts the authority of the Bible. If a person initiates a conversation with us and almost immediately asks us what we think the Bible states about this matter, it is important, I believe, to resist the temptation to show people how bright and knowledgeable we are. Rather, we might more helpfully say something very simple, like, "Why do you ask?" as a way of turning the conversation back to that person's needs and feelings. Or we might say, "That's a very important question; we'll have opportunities to discuss that later. What I'm interested in now is what led you to come and talk with me and to raise this particular issue."

Our convictions can be a help or a hindrance to effective pastoral counseling, depending on how we express them and on the quality of our relationship with the person with whom we're talking. Therefore, the most helpful beginning point in any act of pastoral counseling is an invitation to the other person to express the most pressing feelings and/or needs of which she or he is aware right at the present moment. Our own minds are to begin as blank as possible in regard to what that need is. We put away any preconceptions of the other person that we might have. We then observe perceptively and listen intently both to the precise words and their explicit meanings as well as to any possible implicit meanings.

Let me illustrate. A young man called me for an appointment. I knew neither him nor any member of his family. When he arrived at my study a few days later, we introduced ourselves and sat down. He appeared to be in his late twenties. I began in the way that I almost always do:

"What is it that led you to come to see me?"

His response was, "Well, I'm gay."

"Yes?" (Simply my invitation for him to go on, since for him to say that he is gay gives me no idea at all why it is important for him to tell me this.

Or we could respond, "It sounds as if your being gay has something to do with your being here. Would you clarify this for me?")

He went on to state in a few sentences his slowly growing awareness as a teenager that he might be gay, and that after a few years he had reconciled himself to this fact.

"But what is the reason that you've come here to tell me this?" (I still have no idea what he's after. Any number of gays or lesbians could begin the way he did and need or want very different things. This has to be our real beginning point.)

He lowered his head, was silent for a few seconds, and then looked up at me with obvious embarrassment:

"My mother wanted me to talk with a minister about it and someone recommended you. She wants me to change." His head was still bowed.

I responded something like the following:

"You seemed embarrassed when you said that." (He nodded.) "But now that you're here, what is it that would be important to *you* to talk about?"

His head popped up. He obviously wasn't expecting this. He paused before responding.

"What do *I* want?" (Another pause.) "Well, they want me to change. I've tried to do that. Heaven knows I've tried. But I know now that I simply can't. What I really want. . . . [pause] I love my parents, and I really want them to accept me and love me for the person I am."

This excerpt of a beginning session suggests both an attitude and a procedure with which to begin counseling with anyone, including lesbians and gays. We're not to have preconceived notions of what the other person needs or wants. Our task is to begin by seeking to understand and helping the other person identify, express, explore, and understand her or his needs. The only productive pastoral counseling in most situations will begin with this type of search. Only after that can we and the other person formulate what it is that we can attempt to do next. In the case of this young man, after a thorough exploration with him of his relationship with his parents, it seemed as if conversations with him and them are called for. It is also appropriate to review with him what being gay was like for him from his teen years to this point and what efforts he had actually made to try to change. It is also not out of line at some point in the process to ask a person something like, "Is there any other aspect of your life or your faith that would be important for you to talk about with me?"

The goals of pastoral counseling, then, are to help a person meet the needs that she or he is aware of, help the person identify other needs than those first disclosed, and assist that person to understand himself or herself more clearly so that he or she can make responsible decisions about his or her behavior. We as pastoral counselors are aware that this process always takes place between the person in need and ourselves, representatives of God and the church. That person is aware of it just as we are. The process as a *whole* is a demonstrative proclamation of the Word of God, the love of God being acted out for the person. In addition, in this process, persons often become aware of their need to receive the grace of God, to be forgiven, to find their faith in (that is, commitment to) God increased. This does not happen for everyone with whom we talk any more than all people respond in these ways to effective, powerful, faithful preaching. But they are never totally untouched, either positively or negatively, by the encounter.

PASTORAL COUNSELING WITH TEENAGERS

The minister's talking with teenagers about issues concerning their sexuality are times of unique challenge and opportunity. By teenagers I mean here the period just before or at puberty to seventeen or so. In the context of discussing their own sexuality, I include older children who have had experiences of sexual feelings, fantasies, and (sometimes) behavior prior to their reaching puberty, as well as those seventeen or even a bit older by a few years whose sexual identities are not clearly established. This older group may be characterized by a variety of sexual feelings and experiences, including some who have had very few sexual feelings and fantasies at all. Most of these older teens and young adults feel as if they are not where they "ought" to be or are going to be sexually and socially. Their self-image and sexual orientation are characterized by uncertainty.

Of course, very few of those in the early years of adolescence would come to a pastor on their own initiative (and not too many of the older ones, either), though some may and do. It is important to keep in mind the variety of feelings with which they come, usually doing so because their parents suggested it or exerted a great deal of pressure on them to talk with their pastor. Whether under pressure or by their own desires, they are usually very anxious about discussing their experiences with *anybody*, and would be especially anxious about discussing almost anything personal with a pastor. If they are under parental pressure to come, we can expect them to be resentful and angry in varying degrees. Even though resentment may be focused on the parent(s), it is almost universal that some of it would initially be directed at us, usually expressed in resistance to the process.

Therefore, the first order of business is to get these feelings out into the open with words. If you notice something about the facial expression, body language, or tone of voice, you might say:

"You look [or, sound] uptight."
"You look as though you'd rather be somewhere else."
"You look as if you're very angry."
Or just a simple, "How are you feeling about being here?"

Then help the young person talk about it.

"Tell me what your anxiety is about."

"At whom are you angry?"

"Is some of that anger also directed at me?"

Then, "Tell me more about that."

In the course of the discussion of feelings, the reason for their talking to us and some of what they're going to be talking about will come out as well.

They're also probably going to be suspicious. Is the pastor in collusion with their parents? What if their parents already told the pastor? What's the pastor going to tell their parents? What is the pastor going to *do* to them?

We'll get nowhere at all unless at the beginning we help the young person acknowledge their feelings about being there and then respond to their feelings and any suspicion that they might have. The teenager might also wonder, "What's the minister going to think about me? What sort of relationship will it be?" In regard to the issue of what the pastor will think about him or her, an immediate reassurance of "Of course I'll think well of you no matter what" will probably not be heard so that in the young person's mind the issue of the relationship is immediately resolved. Much better would be something like, "Well, we'll see how this works out. We can't go through a process like this without there being changes in both of us. We can just check it out as we go along. If you're ever concerned about our relationship at any point, you can ask me about it."

In regard to the matter of confidentiality, you can state clearly, "I will never reveal anything that is said between us without talking with you about it first and getting your permission. The only things that I will be compelled to reveal, if you yourself are not willing to do it, is if you are planning to kill yourself or do bodily harm to someone else." Since pastors are committed to work for the person's best interest, we know that telling other people what is said in a confidential conversation is usually not for his or her best interest. But it's also not for the person's best interest if she or he attempts suicide or is planning to attack someone else physically.

Most parents are deeply concerned about their children, and they have a right to know how their children are doing and what they may do to help. For example, if the young person is still living at home and still in school, I'll ask, "Have you told your parents that you're talking to me about this, or even that you are talking to me at all?" If the young person responds, "Yes, but not what about," you may well respond, "I'm glad that you've let them know that you're seeing me. I think you've done the right thing." The parents don't necessarily need to know what about right at this point. If the young person has not told them at all, "Well, at some point it may be best to discuss it with them. If we need to, you and

I can talk more about that. If your parents put a lot of pressure on you to tell them about details of what's going on, I don't mind talking with them and telling them that right at this time the most important thing they can do is not push you. Very likely at some time in the future you may be able to discuss some of the issues with them."

We need to be very sensitive to a young person's anxiety about the parents' finding out. We would not be taking the person seriously if we just brush these concerns aside. What I've been talking about here is not to be understood as a prepared speech that we might give at the beginning of all first counseling sessions. It's simply to lay out two frequent major concerns of young people (and often older ones as well) that need to be dealt with in a way that is honest, relieving, confidence-building, and encouraging. Most of the time, this is done in a give-and-take fashion early in the first conversation, and then raised at the end of that session to check out the young person's understanding of these two issues. There will be no useful conversation unless we provide some assurance of confidentiality and of our continuing "outside the counseling" relationship with them.

As I was writing this section, the headline of an Ann Landers column in the morning paper caught my attention, so I read the letter to which she was responding.

> For the past few months I have been thinking about killing myself. . . . I am fifteen and feel so alone. I am scared. I feel worthless. The problem is that I am absolutely certain that I am gay.

Landers correctly encouraged him to ask a "teacher, counselor, or family doctor" to recommend someone he could talk to. It might be interpreted as noteworthy that she did not include a minister. You might think of some reasons that she did not do this. If this boy were talking with you (lonely, scared, feeling worthless), and after a lengthy conversation having the experience of being understood, of trusting you, although everything is not resolved, he would no longer be alone or feel so worthless and frightened. That in itself lessens the intensity of the suicidal feelings.

However, if suicidal feelings are a part of the young person's response, the parents will need to know just as soon as possible, because they are among the significant persons who can help intervene to reduce the feelings, or if not reduce the feelings, to prevent the attempt. The pastor or some other counselor can guide them in their understanding of their role. The issue of suicide will be discussed in more detail later.

A major result of the first and possibly other pastoral conversations is that the minister can make an initial and tentative assessment in regard to whether the young person is really gay or not. The fifteen-year-old boy who wrote to Ann Landers, "I am absolutely certain that I am gay," might be correct in saying that he *is* gay, or he may be a part of that vast number of people, including many of us, who have been *absolutely* certain about something, but have also been wrong. We may expect that most younger teens and even some older ones are not at all sure of the meaning of sexual fantasies involving persons of the same sex or of those involving adults, usually themselves heterosexual (often teachers at school or Sunday school, Scout leaders, coaches, etc.). They are similarly often lacking in understanding the meaning of the mutual masturbation, some other sexual activity or excitement in physical closeness, or even a specific relationship with someone of the same sex. They often lack an understanding of what it means to be homosexual.

Therefore, very specific information needs to be elicited by the pastor as a means of assisting the young person to see in much more detail a more complete picture of the young person's life. This picture may guide the minister in deciding what step or steps are to be taken next. There are a number of items of information to get out into the open, either by direct question through the other person's initiative, or by eliciting them by empathetic responses, open-ended questions, or simply inviting the person to share more detail.

1. What is the present age of the young person? The younger the person, the greater the possibility that the person's sexual feelings and fantasies and their real life object are still in a state of flux. Her or his experiences may or may not mean that the person is lesbian or gay.

2. At what age did the person first begin to experience him or herself as gay or lesbian? This is an important question in a number of ways, but the immediate one is the matter of possible suicide attempts (again, see the next section).

3. What were the details of the first actual experience?

4. Were the feelings (or attraction to some specific person) always related to persons of the same sex, or were there sometimes feelings toward and attraction to persons of the other sex as well? Were these feelings directed toward an adult or someone about the same age, or both?

5. Does the person now have feelings toward persons of the other sex? Does he or she ever date someone of the other sex? What is the young person's experience of those relationships?

6. What situations tend to arouse the homosexual feelings?

7. Have all or most of the person's sexual feelings resulted from someone else's "coming on" to him or her?

8. Has there actually been sexual activity with a person or persons of either sex or has his or her sexual life been primarily or exclusively fantasy? Give some examples of the fantasies.

9. If there were actual physical experiences, how old was the youth?

Where was that first experience on a continuum of pleasure to displeasure?

10. When the person was a child, did she or he have experiences of being different from others of the same sex?

11. What have been the major sources of the person's dissatisfaction, conflict, anger, anxiety, and sadness in his or her life?

12. What have been the major sources of satisfaction, pleasure (other than sexual), and sense of security in his or her life?
(In 11 and 12, listen especially for references to one or both of the person's parents and/or stepparents and other close members of his or her family.)

13. Is the young person sexually active with others now? About how many different persons and about how often?
(If there are either a number of different people or a considerable frequency of sexual activity or both, we need to restrain ourselves from jumping in too quickly with our discussion of the dangers of sexual promiscuity and the value of Christian morality in regard to sex. These are not inappropriate at all and eventually will come out, but the way into it is probably simply to ask the young person at this point how he or she feels about such sexual activity. Of course, we have to realize that some number of young people will merely lie to a minister in response to this question, but the truth may come out later. There is no need to push too hard about it now.)

14. Is the young person a part of a closely knit group of other lesbian or gay youth, or does he or she have a number of very close friends who are not gay or lesbian?

15. Does the young person know of other persons in his or her family, past and present, who are gay or lesbian? (The physiological research in chapter 2 suggests that if a number of persons in the present and past family have been gay, there is a greater likelihood that a young person having sexual attraction to persons of the same sex is actually gay.)

16. If not mentioned by the young person, always ask if he or she has thought about suicide.

Although these essential areas of exploration have, with the exception of number 15, developed mainly out of my own experience, they are almost identical with many suggested by Wilson, who has additional ones in his list of assessment criteria both for young people and adults, as well as a very useful discussion of them.[10] There may be other areas of investigation that may occur to you, growing out of your own personal and professional experience and as conversation develops with the young person. These questions I have listed are not to be thought of as "quickie" questions and short answer style. Rather, they are the attempt to get a detailed picture of that which has produced sexual confusion or has influenced the person's self-definition. There could well be rather long discussions on the basis of certain questions, including discussing the relevance of each of the questions. This would mean that all of the questions could not be raised in the first session. At least a second session would be required, and probably more.

On the basis of a thorough discussion of these questions and what they elicit from the young person, the pastor is seldom if ever at a point of stating with confidence that the person *is* homosexual or heterosexual. However, in the pastor's own mind, there may well be a lean toward one or the other conclusion. The way into additional evaluation might be for the pastor to ask, "How do you think and feel about yourself as a result of our exploration into your life?"

The young person's responses might be one of the following or even others:

"Well, I think I might not be gay after all," or
"All of this makes me pretty sure that I'm gay," or
"I think I'm just as mixed up as ever."

Don't be too excited, disapproving, disappointed, or dismayed, whatever the response may be. Headway has been made to assist the young person's understanding of him or herself; a trusting relationship with an adult has been established. The stage is set for later additional pastoral conversations or for a referral to a professional psychotherapist or both. The last part of the process of these conversations is full of opportunities and pitfalls for the pastor. The pastor has gone this far with the young person in a sensitive and noncondemnatory way and demonstrated understanding of the young person's responses, stimulating the young person to explore his or her feelings, experiences with others (not just sexual experiences), nonerotic friendships with both sexes; sexual feelings, fantasies, and behavior; relationship with parents; the young person's self-image; and suicidal feelings that might be present.

For myself, and I believe for most pastors, the safest and most helpful course of action at this point would be referral to a competent and trusted psychotherapist and continued contact with the young person by the pastor. The psychotherapist should be well-trained in working with adolescents. Should the therapist be gay or lesbian? If a person meets the other requirements just mentioned, there may often be value in this in some instances. Should it be male with male, female with female? There can be advantages in this also, but I believe that other characteristics of a therapist are usually more important. However, the preference of the young person should also be taken seriously here. It should be a person who has no emotional stake in whether the young person is gay/lesbian or heterosexual and have no bias as to the outcome of therapy, only wanting the young person to develop into the best that that young person can be.

A number of people will want a therapist who is a Christian. If the therapist's faith is well assimilated into her or his personality and expresses itself in compassion and desire for the well-being of the young person, this could be extremely helpful, *if* the therapist has all of the prerequisites I've already mentioned. Being a Christian does not substitute for being well-trained in working with adolescents, for example. It is not a substitute for supervised training that produces a professional who does not allow his or her unconscious needs to exploit the young person and distort the relationship. There are outstanding psychotherapists who are neither Christian nor practicing Jew, who have tremendous respect for the faith of those with whom they are working. They can also assist the person to utilize faith in his or her self-understanding and decision-making.

Naturally it is useful if the minister knows several psychotherapists personally. I recognize the difficulty of this in rural areas, very small towns, and in most smaller churches in the city. I've been there. Clergy who need to make referrals must often rely on a trusted contact person. I can remember, early in my ministry, that I had to refer some people to professionals without any personal knowledge or personal recommendations and simply pray for both therapist and the person referred. There are ways of gaining this personal knowledge, however, by becoming active in mental health associations and councils on alcoholism and attending workshops dealing with various aspects of human behavior and human difficulties that are led by professionals. Such opportunities are accessible, though not usually as readily, outside of metropolitan areas.

Issues Related to Suicide

Few clergy with whom I have talked about their pastoral relationships with people have been fully aware of their crucial role in detecting suicidal feelings and/or talking with these distressed people openly and in detail about those feelings, making a preliminary evaluation of lethality potential, and thus being a significant front line of defense in the prevention of suicides and suicide attempts. It has been too frequently a clergy (and generally human) proclivity to ignore or minimize what people say about their feelings of depression or despair, not feeling able to go on, etc. We seem to be afraid of engaging people in such conversations, as if we will make things worse for them, or for *ourselves.*

What if the fifteen-year-old letter writer had said to us in private, "For the last few months I have been thinking about killing myself. . . . I am absolutely certain that I am gay"?

We have two options if we intend to be responsible. One, we can immediately say something like, "You're feeling so desperate that you're thinking about killing yourself," or "Tell me more about your feelings of wanting to kill yourself."

Or, two, we may respond to his belief, perhaps accurate, perhaps not, that he is gay. "Tell me what's led you to the conviction that you're gay." If we choose the latter option at this point, which is entirely legitimate, then we must be absolutely certain that before we finish talking with him in this session we say (unless he has brought it up again himself), even if we have to interrupt the flow of conversation on any other issue, "We don't have too much longer to talk today, but I wanted to be sure that before we stopped we talked about your feelings of wanting to kill yourself. What's that been like for you?"

We need, of course, to do this with any person of any age, without fail! But there are important reasons that we give particular attention to teenage boys who are or think they are gay. They are definitely a high risk group. We've been aware for a number of years of the rising rate of suicide among youth and young adults, and that rather consistently about three times as many boys as girls kill themselves. Let me give you a more detailed picture of those male teenagers who are gay or who believe themselves to be gay.

One researcher has reported that two-thirds of a sample of U.S. psychiatrists believed that the self-injurious acts of homosexual adolescents were more serious and lethal than those of their heterosexual peers.[11] *The Report of the Secretary's Task Force on Youth Suicide* estimated that gay adolescents were two to three times more likely than their peers to attempt suicide.[12] Gary Remafedi and colleagues studied 137 males between fourteen and twenty-one years of age, with 88 percent identifying themselves as gay and 12 percent as bisexual. Thirty percent of the youth reported at least one suicide attempt, and almost 50 percent of the attempters reported more than one. The average age at the time of the suicide attempt was 15.5 years. Almost half of them made their first attempt in the year that they first identified themselves as gay, with most of the other attempts following soon after. Fifty-four percent of all of the attempts (not just first attempts) were in the moderate to high lethality range. The *younger the person* and the *younger the age of self-labeling* as gay, the more likely he was to make an attempt. Interestingly, each year that goes by without the individual's self-labeling, the odds of a suicide attempt diminished by 80 percent. Many of the youth had made multiple attempts, and multiple attempts are associated with later suicide.[13]

Lacking a young person's explicit report of having suicidal feelings, in addition to a homosexual experience at an early age, early age of self-labeling, and references to previous attempts, a report of illegal drug use or heavy use of prescription drugs would indicate a higher risk. If the pastor is unclear about the possibility of depression, listen carefully to the young person's statements about feeling lonely, unworthy, or a burden to the family, or thinking a lot about death, and ask in more detail about each one. Then it is important that you go on to say, "People who say a number of things like you've said to me are often thinking about killing themselves. I wonder if you're thinking about that."

When such a statement is made in a matter-of-fact way, most people will respond quite honestly. There's no need to fear that you might suggest suicide to them when they would not have thought of it themselves. Never make light of any reference to suicide at any time in any way. Always treat it seriously, but without becoming panicky. Explain your concern about the young person's life, the need for the parents to know, and your own willingness to discuss the matter with the parents. Never (I mean *never*) attempt pastoral counseling with *any* person who is thinking of suicide unless the person is also seeing a qualified professional psychotherapist for an evaluation of lethality potential and for treatment. For young people, this inevitably includes the parents. Never waver from this position! Often the person will need medication, so a psychiatrist would be the preferable referral (or a clinical psychologist in a state in which he or she may legally prescribe medication and admit to a hospital if necessary). If under the primary care of a mental health professional, there can also be a very useful role for a minister's continued focused conversations with the person.[14]

By this time, whether it has been necessary to discuss issues related to suicide or not, it is highly probable that the young person is not feeling the intensity of anxiety that he or she did at the beginning of the conversation, increasingly trusts the minister, and senses that she or he has an ally in this representative in the community of faith. The young person no longer feels so socially isolated because of her or his homosexual feelings and/or experiences, although the pastor does not fully make up for a lack of peer friends. Everything is not resolved, far from it. But there is more hope because of the pastor's genuine care and skill in eliciting the young person's story and his or her feelings, and because the young person has not experienced the condemnation that was probably expected in the first place. In addition, the young person likely has a clearer picture of himself or herself. The probability of immediate suicide or suicide attempt is diminished. Still, a referral to a psychotherapist is imperative.

The Christian Faith and Sexuality

But what has been discussed up to this point isn't all that needs to be talked about, is it? What does it mean to be a Christian when one is in the midst of confusion about one's sexual identity or even believes oneself to be gay or lesbian? The acceptance of the pastor to this point should have communicated God's acceptance. But it is important to make explicit God's role in the person's life. If the young person hasn't raised the question himself or herself, the minister should now move into it.

"With all the struggles and questions and sexual feelings and wondering what all this means for you, I wonder if you've also thought about what role God plays in this part of your life."

Once again, listen carefully and respond to what the young person says. Even though she or he may feel separated from God, or that God has no role in his or her confusion and temptations, the pastor needs to affirm at some appropriate point before the conclusion of the first conversation that God is in fact surrounding the youth with the love that penetrates into *all* areas of her or his life.

But God's active love for them is not the same thing as approval for everything that they *do*. If the young person not only has had genital sex with others but has continued to do so, the pastor's responsibility is to raise with the young person a consideration of God's response to this kind of behavior, the damage that it does to the youth's growth in maturity of self-image and relationships, and what it might be doing to those with whom she or he has been having sex. Promiscuity, whether homosexual or heterosexual, is a violation of God's purposes for us in sexual expression. I want to be clear at this point. I believe that there is no reason to put the behavior *exclusively* in terms of homosexuality. Sexual expression, homosexual or heterosexual, prior to or apart from a mature relationship of love is not God's intention for human beings. Maturity implies readiness to make a life commitment to one another and the awareness of some of the major issues in what life commitment means. To continue to oppose God's will in one's sexual behavior is to continue to damage our relationship with God.

This conversation can be done as a natural and relevant continuation of our earlier conversation of the feelings that brought the young person to us in the first place. It can be done in a serious and caring and non-condemnatory but clear way.

ADULTS

Several active clergy over the years as well as a number of seminary students have asked for appointments with me. After we have been seated, they have usually begun with a simple statement:

"You've known me for several (or many) years, but I want you to know something else about me that's very important to me. I am lesbian (gay)."

The active clergy have usually gone on to tell me in greater detail about their original self-discovery and what this has meant in their lives, usually considerable struggle, some complications. They have expressed confidence in their relationship with God and their desire to continue as clergy, well aware of the risks. Some have worked this out constructively with their spouses within the continuing marriage or with love-affirming divorce, although there are certainly times of anger and distress.

Neither these students nor clergy have seemed to be asking anything explicitly of me other than my simply listening and receiving what they have said. I hear no references to problems, no asking for help, nothing else. Why is the person telling us this?

Part of the answer depends on who we are. Have we preached and/or taught that homosexuality is a sin? What attitude have we conveyed when we've done that? Have we declared authoritatively, as the chief elected officer of a major denomination recently did, "We believe that homosexuality is a free choice, and therefore under *all* conditions is a sin"? Or have we shown that we've honestly studied the issues and have still come to the conclusion that sexual behavior by homosexual persons is a sin, but we also convey Christian compassion and a desire to understand as we talk with the person? The person's motives could be different for coming out to different ones of us.

A fascinating coming out and the response to it is described by Mel White.[15] White is an evangelical Christian, a talented writer and film maker, who slowly began to recognize his feelings for certain other males. He had had such feelings prior to marriage but was also in love with the young woman whom he married. They were committed to each other, had children, had a good family life. But after years of sincere struggle, not only prayer but unsuccessful therapy of various kinds, he finally submitted to the reality of his being gay. His talent and his involvement with evangelical Christians was so well known that over the years he was asked to be a "ghost writer," a writer of speeches, some sermons, and the "autobiographies" of several well-known evangelists, all but one of whom had preached vehemently against homosexuality. When White finally decided to make his sexual orientation openly known, he wrote a letter to each one of these evangelists with whom he had been so close. He detailed his struggle, his dawning realization that he was, in fact, gay; he reaffirmed his Christian faith; he asked for a personal appointment with each of them so that they might discuss all of this in more detail face to face. *He received not a single answer of any kind* from these very well-known preachers.

White's purpose was clear, to be honest, to be more fully and accurately known. But I suspect that part of his purpose also may have been the hope that these men might come to a more realistic and therefore more loving view of who gay people are. But they seemed to be absolutely closed.

Regardless of the odds of success, some gays and lesbians tell certain ministers in order to educate, and some number of ministers do begin to change their views in the direction of understanding and kindness. Even those ministers who honestly believe that homosexual *behavior* is sin need to consider what their response would be if someone whom they have known, liked, appreciated, and respected revealed his or her homosexuality.

Throughout our ministry, most of us have had or should anticipate experiences of various kinds that properly lead us to consider new ideas, new opportunities in ministry, new ways of relating well to more people. Often this new growth comes rather slowly, with a number of gentle leadings. But sometimes it comes to us with a crashing impact and can produce considerable discomfort for us. Growing toward maturity in ministry is what all of this is about. All of us have experienced this. Discovering lesbian and gay friends is among the experiences that have potential to stimulate our growth.

Sometimes, as I have suggested, this is the gay or lesbian's purpose. Whether it was the purpose of those who have come to me, I don't know. But it has had an effect, beginning back with George thirty-three years ago in the parish, and continuing with the first several clergy and seminary students who spoke with me and continue to do so.

Helping When Needed

Have some of these people who are "just telling us" also been asking for help in some way, but have been reluctant to be explicit, don't know how to present it, or are afraid? They begin, but they need a sense of how we are responding, what we think of them, some help in clarifying what it is they want.

But what is the person's intent when he or she is merely telling us about being lesbian or gay? Even listening with that combination of believing what the person says along with our trained pastoral counseling suspicions, we hear no problem. We hear no request of any kind. Our most helpful response is to attempt to elicit their reason for their revealing themselves to us. It's really very simple. "I wonder why you're telling me this about yourself." This simple statement communicates our willingness to engage ourselves further with them and is an invitation for them to say what it is they want from us.

There are a number of possibilities. Young adults may want help in clarifying to themselves whether they really are gay or not (more men than women have raised this question with me). The suggested areas of investigation listed earlier for youth are appropriate here as well. There can be values for the pastor and the young man or woman discussing these in some detail. For most, however, although helpful in establishing a relationship with a minister and increased self-understanding, it will often not be a substitute for that person's talking with a professional psychotherapist.

If the person is specifically asking for help in getting rid of the homosexual feelings, that is, becoming heterosexual, when the primary indications are that he or she is gay or lesbian, the pastor can and should offer herself or himself as a supportive friend and also as a representative of God. My personal opinion, based on my own experiences, the experience of a number of other clergy, and the experience of most psychotherapists, is that not only is such a change an impossible goal for us with that person, but that we may actually do the person harm if we try.

Our most effective role, that for which we are trained, is to be the best pastor we can be to the person, cultivate the congregation to accept gays and lesbians within the Christian fellowship for study, service, and worship, and refer those persons who wish to explore their sexual orientation in detail to the most competent psychotherapist we can find.

Even then, most psychotherapists who are willing to work with persons with an initial focus on their homosexual orientation will not have as their goal the changing of that person to heterosexual. In fact, in August 1997 the Counsel of Representatives of the American Psychological Association (APA) clarified treatment guidelines for mental health professionals based on the current knowledge about homosexuality as a sexual orientation and about the limitations of psychotherapy that attempts to change that orientation to heterosexual. The APA resolution also detailed the therapists' ethical responsibilities to their clients.[16] Assumed in that document, though not explicitly stated, is the accumulation of evidence giving rise to serious doubts about the possibility of such change, although a very few therapists do claim such results. This is not to say, however, that there can't be considerable potential value to persons in exploring in detail with a competent therapist their sexual orientation in relation to other areas of their lives. There certainly is such potential.

It probably also needs to be said, since I both read and hear it from time to time, that there are a number of Christians who believe that lesbians and gays who really want to change and who are willing to give their lives fully to Christ can be changed by God and can become heterosexual. There are groups of Christian people who have organized themselves to facilitate such a ministry. I have read the testimonies of a few people who claim to have been changed in this way. I want to try to continue to have an open mind about the possibility of changing from homosexuality to heterosexuality through conversion. But nevertheless, I remain skeptical, and the source of my skepticism is, I believe, not just a preconceived bias (I formerly believed that such sexual orientation change could come about through dependence upon God and/or through psychotherapy), but comes out of numerous reports by many of those who have sought the conversion road themselves.

These reports are by those who later said that what came out of their experience of Christ and the support of a group who claimed that through such an experience gays and lesbians could become heterosexual was a *repression* of their homosexual feelings, a change in their *lifestyle* so they no longer felt *driven* by those feelings. This new experience fit their understanding of how they should be living their Christian faith. But these persons were not experiencing *heterosexual* feelings either. Others have reported that the homosexual feelings were not taken away, not even repressed, but merely that they were, if single, empowered to live a celibate life, which they understood to be the will of God for themselves.

I'm not at all critical of the role of these experiences in people's lives. In fact, I celebrate them, *if* the persons involved experience more joy, more genuine (*agape*) love, a greater sense of following God's will. But they are not reports of being *changed* from a homosexual orientation to a heterosexual orientation.

In Search of a Blessing

Another possible reason that some lesbians and gays might come to us and simply tell us of their sexual orientation is for their own psychological and spiritual well-being. Some merely want someone whom they know and who is in some way an "authority" figure (teacher, pastor, dean, etc.) to know the fuller truth about them. Others specifically want an ordained minister. There is always some risk in telling, although they have usually had enough experience of the person to minimize that risk and have some trust in the person's response. When the acceptance is clearly expressed in some way, they seem to have a sense of relief, of calm, of being more fully understood and still accepted.

"Pastor, I came by just to tell you something about myself that you may not know. I'm lesbian (gay)."

If the pastor responds with acceptance and encouragement, perhaps with a simple, "Tell me how it is that you decided to share this with me," the person has experienced a blessing, even though it's not been a formal one and the name God has not been used. Just remember that to most of those who are telling us this, we are the representatives of God, so the blessing *in God's name* is always implicit.

When I've been involved in such a brief exchange, useful in and of itself, I now look back and wonder, should there have been something else? Might I not be more helpful if I also then said, "Is there anything else that you want (or feel the need) to tell me about this?" or, "Would you be willing to tell me more about this part of your life?" I believe that such a question is not unnecessarily intrusive; it shows interest; and perhaps it would be received as an invitation to share more when the person would not otherwise have offered it.

But no more than this at this time! A persistent searching for a "problem" when the persons are not aware of any can communicate to them that we assume that if they are gay or lesbian there are bound to be problems. This in turn communicates a prejudice against who they are and negates their purpose in coming merely to make our relationship more open and honest, thus blessing us both.

Blessings are making a comeback in many of our Protestant denominations, which either never really had or somewhere along the line have lost the practice of explicit blessings that can make Christian life more meaningful. They have more typically been found in group liturgy. Blessings, other than at baptisms and weddings, were never a part of my experience of church life as a child, adolescent, young adult, or even minister for many years. I believe now that they can be a powerful stimulus to Christian living. I deeply regret my many lost opportunities as a minister to add to the other persons' and my own Christian life by not being aware of blessings.

When a person comes to us and tells us of being lesbian or gay, just because he or she values our relationship and wants us to know (or, in fact, is *seeking* a blessing but is not using the word), we ask if there is more that they want or need to tell us. If yes, we encourage their expression so we can listen and respond appropriately. Then, as well as when there is nothing else the person wants to say, it seems to me to be appropriate to offer a blessing. We can say whatever is appropriate to our relationship with the person, to what she or he has said. It can be very simple.

We place our hands on the person's head or take the person's hand and say something like, "I bless you in the name of God, Father of our Lord Jesus Christ" (or use the words of the Trinity) and perhaps offer a short prayer. The prayer may be for the person and her or his relationship with God and the relationship between the person and yourself. Follow what you have learned in your church tradition as well as the immediate leading of the Spirit.

I'm well aware that many clergy will not be able to do this because of the deep conviction they have that it would not be morally right to bless a gay or lesbian person. Let's examine more closely, though, what a blessing is and what it is we could be blessing. When we "bless," we confirm God's love for that person.

Now, in what context would this blessing be given? The person has taken the initiative to speak *trustingly* to a representative of God and the community of faith. Why would a person do that? The person desires to be known to us as he or she really is, no longer hiding behind a façade. It's a courageous step—offering himself or herself to one who represents the church. It comes out of the person's awareness of a spiritual need. It's a way of stating, "God knows me for who I am. I now want to be known by you as a person and as the designated representative of the community of faith." Is this, understood in this way, not an act worthy of blessing as blessing has been defined? Remember, the person has said, "This is who I *am*," seldom having recounted everything that she or he has been *doing* prior to this moment. In fact, very few of us would dare to ask God or our minister/confessor to bless *everything* that we have *done*. We want a confirmation of God's love now that can influence our future. It is the *person* and this act of *self-revelation* and our *relationship* with one another and *God's love* for the person that is being affirmed in the blessing.

The Blessing of Gay/Lesbian Relationships

I realize that there are some clergy who will not want to read this section at all (*even* if they have gotten this far in the book). Others will read reluctantly, skeptically, and with resistance about that which seems to you to be a radical violation of the Scripture and traditional Christian belief. However, I pray that you might continue to read and that your mind might be open to considering what I am proposing, knowing that all of us will never believe alike and will never agree on certain acts of Christian ministry.

I would imagine that only a tiny percentage of clergy have ever explicitly blessed particular gay couples and lesbian couples. I am sure that very few have ever been asked to do so. I haven't. Couples themselves have been very reluctant to consider it. Large numbers of clergy believe that the Bible prohibits such a blessing and a number of major denominations have statements that would call into question their clergy's participating in such a service. Some clergy might understand that such a blessing could be a legitimate act of ministry but emotionally could not bring themselves to do it. The blessing might get mixed up with the idea of Christian marriage, a basis on which many Christian clergy could not consider it. Some, on what logical basis I have never understood nor even heard articulated, would see it as leading to "the breakdown of the family." (I can't resist the impulse to make the side comment that the breakdown of the family to the extent to which we have it today seems to me to have been totally the responsibility of heterosexual people.)

Gay and lesbian relationships cover the same spectrum in every regard as those of heterosexual persons, including the persons' level of emotional maturity, religious commitment, and other variables. I grew up, including my "growing up" after age twenty-one and after becoming a minister and pastor of a church in an age when the accepted understanding of gays (not a word used then, of course) was that they all had serious developmental problems that had left them on a level of emotional and social immaturity. As a result of this immaturity, most of them were sexually promiscuous, or at least had a lengthy series of love relationships (just another form of promiscuity). They were, it was thought, simply incapable of a long-term committed relationship of love. And, in fact, we never saw such long-term relationships. This doesn't mean that they didn't exist, but we just didn't see them. There were, of course, good reasons for their invisibility. There were dangers of several kinds for them. In addition, if we didn't *see* them, we didn't have to *deal with* them.

The myth of their universal immaturity and pathology was exploded decades ago.[17] Nevertheless, the usual social lag of new information, however well founded the information might be, was exacerbated in this case because of the massive emotional resistance to the idea that except for the sex of those who stimulated our sexual desire, gays and lesbians as a *group* were *just like us* heterosexuals as a group. But they are, and the reality is that there are lesbian couples and gay couples whose relationships are the *equivalent* of marriage, whether there has been a ceremony or not. They meet the criteria stated by Gaiser, "committed, loving, and just," and "fidelity, public accountability, and permanency."[18]

Let's look first at different expressions of sexual relationship, reflecting as we do so whether any of this makes a difference to the One who created us as sexual beings, for sexual relationship in mature, committed, loving, faithful relationship. Gays have been severely criticized for frequent one-night stands, pick-ups in gay bars, anonymous sex in which sometimes even the face of the other is not seen, or "quickies" in a public restroom during lunch break, in a car, or in a park before going home to spouse and children. Obviously, criticism of this behavior is clearly justified from a biblical point of view. There can be no debate about that. It has at least in years past been a part of the stereotypical picture of gays, and, of course, some gays still behave this way.

Overlooked in this criticism of gays has been the reality of almost identical sexual behavior on the part of heterosexual men and women, although I certainly don't know nearly as much about women as I do about men. For the unmarried there may be several nights a week with different partners, pick-ups in bars and off the street, as well as persons we know in our usual daily work and social settings. Married men also make pick-ups in bars and drive-by pick-ups of women prostitutes for a quickie before going home to the family, to say nothing of longer lasting sexual affairs outside of marriage. This sexual behavior is clearly and repetitively condemned in the Bible—Old Testament and New Testament.

God's gift of sex is for relationship, for the psychological and spiritual growth of persons in relationship, committed to one another, and made richer by their sexual love. Sex without love, without giving to and receiving from another in other ways, does not contribute to our growth as persons and certainly does not contribute to a deepening relationship to God. Quite to the contrary, it reinforces immaturity, may be physically harmful, violates the "temple of God," which is our body, and builds barriers between us and God. Many gays also have a partner for a while, then break up and have another, then another, and many over a lifetime. Somewhat more complex in procedures, but otherwise similar, are those heterosexual women and men who marry, whose relationship is often enough *blessed* by a representative of the community of faith (although at other times by other designated officials), and who divorce, then remarry, frequently with *another* blessing by a minister, and later divorce. For some, this procedure is repeated a number of times.

While not indiscriminate promiscuity, persons who over a period have a number of partners, whether homosexual or heterosexual, *are* acting out immature needs, contribute to the persistence of that immaturity, and are violating the will of God.

There is no clear evidence that emotional and social immaturity and sexual promiscuity is more of a characteristic of gays and lesbians than it is of heterosexuals. But for obvious reasons, the gays who are usually seen and generalized about are not those in long-term committed relationships. Society seems to have been organized to discourage such relationships by gays and lesbians, and even committed lesbian and gay relationships of love have been condemned. Life commitments need social support, including, for many people, the support of a congregation, and usually involving the blessing of God in the context of a worship service performed by a minister representing the community of faith in his or her act. Where do gays go for such social support, for the blessing of God and church? The answer is clear: to very few churches and very few clergy. The exception is the ministry of the Metropolitan Community Churches and some other individual congregations composed primarily of lesbian and gay persons. I've heard a few lay people and ministers criticize these churches. I'm reminded of the famous evangelist of a couple of generations ago, who when some of his methods were criticized by another minister, replied, "Well, I like the way I'm *doing* it better than the way you all are *not* doing it." As long as we in other congregations are not accepting and loving of *all* persons, the MCC and others are performing ministry for those gays and lesbians who are seeking God.

Yet as time has gone by, many lesbians and gays have become more open about themselves, and we have begun to know a number of them in many of our churches, our businesses and professions, our neighborhood, and for many of us, our own families. Gay and lesbian couples have become less willing to attempt to live in secret. It has become apparent that they can love just as much, with as much commitment, for as long a period of time as heterosexual couples can. Still, large numbers of heterosexual persons have not had the opportunity or taken the opportunity to become aware of this reality, or have had powerful denial that that is the case. But it's true, nevertheless.

A while ago I attended a meeting of Parents and Friends of Lesbians and Gays. Sitting in front of me with their arms on the back of the church pew and coming down around the other's shoulders were two men. When the time came for anyone who wanted to speak to the group to do so, one of these men came forward. He said that he was full of joy as he and his partner were celebrating their thirtieth anniversary on that day. The speaker had been a Baptist minister, and the two of them had daily devotions and prayer together and attended a Baptist church.

We have known an openly gay couple in a church we're familiar with who have been together for many years. We have other friends who are gay couples of many years' standing. Many families have such couples as a part of their families. We've seen almost unbelievable expressions of fidelity by gay men whose life partners of many years were dying of AIDS: daily visits to the hospital, long periods of tender care in the home, physical exhaustion, emotional strain, and the pain of seeing a loved one dying so slowly, with serious combinations of symptoms that others might view as impossible to witness. Should not such love and commitment be affirmed and blessed?

Can we really believe that God makes *no* distinction between sexual promiscuity and life commitments of love and fidelity? We certainly have no difficulty in making such a distinction when thinking of heterosexual persons. That is absolutely explicit in the Bible. But even for those who believe that all sexual relations between men and between women are wrong, are sin, is there not really a difference between promiscuous sex without meaningful personal relationship and sex with one love partner in a committed covenantal relationship?

Remember, the Bible apparently did not know and certainly did not speak to the issue of gays and of lesbians whose relationships are *comparable* to that of marriage in that there is genuine *philia/agape* love, as well as *eros*, between partners who have consciously and seriously committed themselves to each other for life. Where the Bible is silent on important matters, as it is here, what do we do? We attempt, through serious biblical study and prayer, to apply the relevant passages of the Scripture to the issues at hand.

As one source of our judgment concerning lesbians and gays, let's look at 1 John 4:7, 16. "Beloved, let us love one another; for love is of God and [the one] who loves is born of God and knows God. . . . God is love, and [the one] who abides in love abides in God, and God abides in [that person]."

There is, of course, a danger in using this text with a couple "in love," whether heterosexual or homosexual. Obviously, the author is not meaning *eros* (sexual love, which is never used in the New Testament at all). He is emphasizing the love (*agape*) that Christians should have for one another in the church, since God through Christ has shown divine love for us. (Only *agape* is used throughout 1 John.) But certainly we realize that in a relationship in which there is *eros,* and *agape* is also man-ifested, then those persons' love can be said to be from God. This is the assumption of the Christian wedding ceremony. *Eros* tends to be assumed as a dynamic force within and between most of the persons coming to be married. The ceremony in most churches then goes on to ask about their *agape* (the commitment to and acting for the well-being of the other): "Will you love, comfort, honor, keep in sickness as well as health?" and each person states, "I take you for better, for worse; for richer, for poorer; in sickness and in health, till death us do part." This is *agape* love. First John 4:12 states: "If we love (*agapomen*) one another, *God* abides in us. . . ." And verse 16: "God *is agape,* and [one] who abides in *agape* abides in God, and God abides in that person."

Actually, many commentators warn us about making too much of any distinction between the two words for love in the New Testament (*agape* and *philia,* the latter often thought of as affection friends have for one another). *Agape* is the quite distinctive New Testament word, and when *philia* is used, while denoting a personal element, it usually con-tains *agape.* Neither has any implication of sexual feeling, but they don't *exclude* the possibility of *eros* either. Too many couples say they love one another when *eros* is predominant, but either by conscious design or by immaturity have no intent or capacity for *agape,* nor even *philia,* except in a temporary sense, when everything "is going my way." Most of us clergy have had misgivings about some fair number of couples who ask us to perform their wedding. We usually have no doubt about their *eros,* but we are quite uncertain of their ability to act out *agape/philia* in their relationship for the rest of their lives. But we go ahead and perform the weddings anyway.

My observations and conversations with and my reading about les-bian and gay couples is that they are as sincere and capable as heterosex-ual couples as far as their capacity for *agape* is concerned. That is, many are capable of it, and some number aren't.

What is the test? What have they demonstrated throughout their lives to this time and in their relationship to show that their love is (1 Corinthi-ans 13) patient and kind, not jealous or self-centered, not ill mannered or selfish or irritable; does not keep a record of wrongs; is not happy with evil, but with the truth; *never gives up?* Its faith, hope, and patience never fail.

Once again I think of the faithful care, tenderness, and commitment of many gays with their partners who are dying of AIDS. Was there ever a love like this? It's like Jesus, who loved to the point of his own death. With these gay men, sexual desire is no longer a motivating part of their relationship. The physical and emotional demands are too great. They are exhausted. There is no respite. But care, tenderness, patience, and commitment remain.

Even though a minister may still believe that the sexual expression of love between lesbians and between gays is sin, could not the commitment of faithful *philia/agape* love be blessed by representatives of the community of faith simply because that kind of love is of God?

Consider the number of Christians, including clergy, who have divorced. Later they develop a committed love relationship with someone of the other sex. They desire that loving, committed relationship to be blessed by the church. But we all know, don't we, Matthew 9:19 (presented from a male point of view only, of course, because men were the only ones who could initiate it then): "Whoever divorces his wife, except for *porneia* ['any kind of unlawful sexual intercourse']¹⁹ and marries another, commits adultery." (Of course, we also know that Mark does not even have the qualification, "except for *porneia*.") Yet in spite of the Matthew and Mark statements, most divorced clergy remarry, and most of the time do so in the church, with another clergy person officiating.

How can we clergy preside at the marriage ceremonies of people who have been divorced, blessing the sexual expression of love in that union, which the Bible condemns? Is it not because, even in the face of sin, we believe that in a committed relationship of love (*philia/agape*) and most of the time along with *eros*, there is God? So how is this different from a lifelong loving committed relationship of gays and lesbians, even though you may also believe that sin is in it? Are not our marriage relationships also accompanied by sin since there is none of us without sin (Rom. 3:23)? Does not God, who *is* Love, and who is found wherever there is *agape*, bless and support the loving, committed unions of gays and of lesbians, just as God can only despise relationless sex, anonymous sex, and "lust only" sex, whether between gays, between lesbians, or between heterosexuals?

PASTORAL MINISTRY TO PERSONS WITH AIDS (PWAs)

A man who had been a friend of mine for several years and a colleague for part of that time phoned me one day. His twenty-nine-year-old son, Don, was gay; he was in the hospital and was dying of AIDS and at least one other AIDS-related disease. He told his father that he would like to talk with a minister. Although raised in the church, he had been alienated from it for about fourteen years, and he didn't even know a pastor. The parents were not related to any local church, either, so they called me. Within forty-five minutes I was in his hospital room. No one else was with him at the time. As I came close to his bed, I told him who I was and that his dad had told me that he'd said he wanted to talk to a minister. I reached out and took his hand. He held on tightly. He was emaciated; his eyes were sunken into his head; his skin was a pasty color. Immediately he said, "Talk to me about God."

What an opening: a minister being asked to talk about God. But by this time in my life I'd learned enough to resist the temptation. (In seminary we had studied a book entitled simply *The Doctrine of God*, which was over five hundred pages long.) I had learned enough to know that God-talk in general or in great undirected detail, is folly. It is relevant and potentially powerful only when focused upon the concrete needs of a particular person.

"Talk to me about God."

"Tell me what you've been thinking about, and what you've been feeling that leads you to want to talk about God."

"I am so afraid."

And he began to tremble. I continued to hold Don's hand. I'm not sure of the exact words that I said next, but I am clear that they were about God's loving presence with the two of us right at that moment. After a bit, he stopped trembling; he relaxed. We began to talk about him, his situation, his awareness that he wouldn't live much longer. I would ask a question. He would respond. And frequently he would ask a question, and I'd respond. I don't think I've ever been with anybody who was as hungry for the reality of God's presence as he. After twenty minutes or so it was obvious that he was tiring rapidly, and I suggested that we stop and that I would come back the next day. He immediately asked me to read from the Bible before I left. I asked him if he had some special passage in mind for me to read. He did—the 23rd Psalm. I read, had prayer with him, and left.

Over the next few weeks I visited with him several times a week. Don usually had a challenge for me as soon as I walked in:

"Tell me more about God."

Another time, as soon as I came in, "Read the Bible to me."

And, "Tell me what heaven's like."

Each time, I would direct him back to his feelings, his concrete experience and needs, and what he had been thinking about, and then in the light of what he said, I would go back to his first request. Throughout all of this time his life partner had been visiting him daily, although only twice while I was there. Though wracked with grief and fear, this other young man, who was HIV-positive himself, was extremely supportive of Don. Don was also blessed by parents whose love and concern for him as a person and as their son with AIDS were not compromised by the fact that he was gay. One or both of them would visit him a couple of times a day.

When AIDS is advanced, as it was in Don, the person may at times forget that you were there the day before. Just reassure him that you were, mention very briefly the key points of the conversation, and quote a verse of the Scripture. Be patient and reassuring that you will not desert him.

After about six weeks, Don died. His physical body was wasted. But he seemed more at peace, his spirit in touch with God.

Of course, gay men are not the only persons who become infected with the Human Immunodeficiency Virus (HIV), but in the United States, several Western European countries, and perhaps some others, they continue to be the majority. HIV can be one of the cruelest destroyers of the human body, the human emotions, and the human spirit. The disease is still relatively new on the scene in the United States and in other Western countries. Probably the first identification of it in the United States was in June 1981. At that time, it was already widespread in several countries in central Africa, almost entirely among *heterosexual* persons. It is still the case worldwide that the majority who are HIV-positive or who have AIDS are heterosexual. However, in the United States the largest number of infected persons quickly appeared in the gay male population, and in 1993 gay men were 53 percent of all cases. Although in 1995 the number of AIDS cases among women was only 19 percent, their number rose 63 percent from 1991 to 1995, compared with a 12.8 percent increase among men. The major source of the women's increase has been intercourse with infected men and infection from previously used needles while injecting drugs.

HIV is contracted primarily by male-female intercourse and anal intercourse with an infected male, the sharing of needles by intravenous drug users of whom at least one is infected, and a transfusion of blood containing the virus, and less frequently by other behaviors and accidents that involve infected blood entering the blood stream of another. In 1992, about one-fourth of infants born to HIV-infected mothers, about 2,000 per year, were also infected. Now as a result of treating many mothers with AZT during pregnancy, fewer than 500 infected infants are born each year. By the end of June 1996, according to the U.S. Centers for Disease Control and Prevention, more than 350,000 Americans had died of AIDS and/or its related opportunistic diseases. It has been the leading cause of death among American males between the ages of 25 and 44, although in 1996 and 1997 the annual number of their deaths from this cause decreased.

At the time of this writing there is no immunization against the disease, although there seems to be progress being made in that direction. There still is no clear-cut *cure*. Some people with AIDS are finding hope in a combination of three medications in current use (AZT, a second generation of protease inhibitors, and a new group called integrase inhibitors), taken regularly in their complex exact proper dosages (numerous doses every day) with the exact proportion of each medication in the exact order they are to be taken at the precise times. In addition to this time-consuming and mentally challenging process of medication, the side effects can be quite unpleasant. But the drugs have extended the lives of many sufferers of the disease for several years, and some hopeful beginnings have been made to reduce the noxious nature of the side effects. Some persons have even experienced a remission of the disease, although the virus itself apparently remains alive. Progress in treatment continues to be made. A recent study reported that over nine months, AIDS patients getting a combination of the protease inhibitor Indinavir, plus AZT and Lamivudine, had half the death rate of those getting just two drugs.[20] Nevertheless, pastoral ministry with persons with AIDS will be needed for a long time to come.

What do we as pastors need in order to be effective caregivers to PWAs?

1. We need to remember that not all PWAs and certainly not nearly all who are HIV-positive but without AIDS are bedridden. The latter group look and function like anyone else. But they are still persons in intense need. Numerous ones of them will be a part of many congregations. Others will be in families who are members of our parish, whether the infected persons attend or not. Family members usually have complex and sometimes conflicting feelings about their loved one if they know about his or her being HIV-positive, and their needs should always be kept in mind by the minister.

2. It is important to realize the great need of the persons for faith in a loving and forgiving God whom *we* represent. Remembering Jesus, we need to be genuinely loving, that is, giving ourselves to persons with great need. (A man in his forties who has AIDS was told eleven years ago that he had six months to live. He states that he has come to see his infection as a "spiritual journey." He goes on to say, "I think what has helped keep me alive is finally learning how to love another human being unconditionally.")[21] We can teach a person to love unconditionally only by our own loving that person unconditionally.

3. Don't be afraid. We can't catch it by breathing the same air the person with AIDS does, using the same spoon to stir our coffee, holding their hand, or touching them in other ways. HIV dies very quickly when exposed to dry surfaces and the open air. (Nevertheless, use reasonable caution; if the PWA *and* if we ourselves have open lacerations or sores, be sure that these do not come into contact.) Therefore, always touch the person: hold his or her hand, put your hand on his or her forehead when you pray, etc. So many persons with AIDS have been treated as pariahs ("untouchables"), often even by their own families. Many of them inevitably have come to feel this way about themselves. Therefore, their being touched in love is a very comforting, affirming experience for them.

I was visiting a young man with AIDS in his hospital room when suddenly the door opened and a very attractive young woman appeared and walked quickly to his bedside. She had a bouquet of flowers in her hand. She bent over and kissed him on the forehead, calling him by name, and then arranged the flowers for him in a glass of water. I was moved to tears by this kiss of affection, especially so when I discovered that she was a nurse who worked in his doctor's office.

4. Be persons of a living and meaningful faith ourselves and have a good knowledge of the location in the Bible of potentially useful passages for reading.

5. Rid ourselves of the need, if we have it, to "sermonize." Simply ask the other to speak about his or her experiences and feelings, listen intently and gain an understanding of *this* PWA's specific needs, and respond appropriately to those particular needs with our words and the words of the Scripture.

6. Visit more and more frequently as the person becomes sicker.

7. Always have a prayer that picks up the person's stated needs and high points of the conversation and present these to God on his behalf.

A potentially very powerful process into which the pastor may lead the person is some combination of relaxation exercises, meditative prayer, meditation focused on a particular verse or word of Scripture, and possibly other forms of meditation with which the pastor may be familiar. There is supportive interaction between these processes, which can potentially open the person to God's presence, often offering some insight or what the person understands as a personal word from God, and sometimes at least a temporary and occasionally longer relief from the pain and other troublesome and debilitating symptoms, increasing confidence in God's love and care. Relaxation alone is peacegiving and may be pain-reducing and strengthening to the person. Although there may be no explicit Christian emphasis in the relaxation exercise, the pastor is seen as a representative of God, and the Christian message is conveyed implicitly. Relaxation is also a necessary precursor as well as a result of the other processes of meditation and prayer. The leadership of the pastor in these processes is also a way of teaching the person to initiate the process for himself or herself. The person becomes capable of relaxing and meditating even when the pastor is not present, and so there is increasingly a strengthening relationship with God as well as the physical benefits that often accompany and/or result from the process.

For persons who do not have AIDS but are HIV-positive, the leading and teaching of relaxation/meditation, especially meditative prayer based on Scripture, are forces in spiritual development and may also have physically strengthening results. Because most HIV-positive persons are working at their jobs, exercising, and going to social events, plays, and perhaps church, we usually are not aware of the anxiety with which they live. In fact, we are usually not even aware that they are HIV-positive. But if we do gain knowledge of their infection, it is important that we make ourselves more available to them than we would otherwise: be willing to investigate with them their feelings and their uncertainty concerning the future, and be in touch with them from time to time but without discomforting them by our being oversolicitous.

It is critical to our own pastoral ministry and to the PWA's or HIV-positive person's sense of comfort with us that we engage ourselves with him or her *without any presumption* as to how the person contracted the disease. If during our conversations and developing relationship, the person tells us that he is gay or that she has been sharing needles with intravenous drug users, effective caring requires that we receive that information like anything else a person tells us, without shock or condemnation. Some of them already tend to feel some type of condemnation in it. Often they will be fearful that we'll pull away from them. By our continuing to engage in significant conversations with them right at the moment and by touching them, we communicate our caring for and commitment to them. In addition, staying with them in their times of extremity is also an assurance to many persons that God cares, God has not abandoned them, God will be with them to the end, and not even death will be able to separate them from the love of God.[22]

Finally, a significant part of our pastoral ministry to PWAs is to enlighten, motivate, and lead individual members or small groups within our congregation to offer themselves in a variety of ways to other community organizations and institutions who are serving PWAs: public clinics, hospitals, specialized counseling centers and programs, and residences for PWAs who have no other place to live. There are increasing numbers, especially in large cities, of the service group called AIDS Interfaith Network. It would be useful for the minister and some representative(s) of the congregation to be in touch with an AIDS Interfaith Network service if there is one in their area.[23]

Pastoral ministry meets more needs of more people if the congregation becomes involved and if use is made of specialized service organizations. A local church could offer its facilities for an AIDS support group or support groups for families of PWAs. These and other congregational ministries are much more in keeping with the ministry of Jesus than a number of other activities that many congregations sponsor.

COMING OUT

One troubling issue a lesbian or gay person may bring to a pastor is that of coming out, to whom is the person going to reveal that she or he is gay. Living with his or her sexual orientation completely a secret from everyone is almost impossible, and attempting to do so is an almost unbearable strain. Most of us who are heterosexual enjoy being with one or two or a group of people who are more or less like us. We need human companionship to be more fully human ourselves, so we get together for a little while with a few people we work with before going home at the end of the workday, visit with friends in the neighborhood, attend church and often are a part of one or more smaller groups in the church, belong to a men's or women's service club or a fraternity or sorority, go home to our families, and so on. With such groups we aren't under a strain to be overly self-protective. Although most of us have some secrets we don't want others to know, it's no great strain to keep them under cover with these friends, these groups. We are a part of the majority. We are open about a number of personal matters with many people and have some substantial amount of understanding and support.

Can you try to imagine what it would be like to be gay or lesbian in our society? At school, at work, going out with the group, being with the family, going to church; being in a Sunday school class; being a member of the Lions, Rotary, Kiwanis, or the Business and Professional Women's Association, not knowing if *anyone* there is like me; believing that practically all of them would reject me and condemn me if they knew my secret. There is so much risk. Gays and lesbians don't receive from these friends, clubs, and associations the relaxation and unrestrained joy and affirmation that we heterosexuals do. There's not much freedom to find gay and lesbian friends within these groups. Is it any surprise that they go to gay bars and to churches whose members and visitors are well-known to be primarily lesbian and gay? They can relax, be themselves, and find acceptance as who they are. But these times are limited. Most lesbians and gays experience an intense need to be openly themselves with members of their families, some of their close colleagues, and friends. But to which ones? How much risk should they take? They talk with one another about it. And some fair number would like to talk with a minister about it, but few do.

If you as a pastor can be a trusted friend (whether you approve of their homosexuality or not), and if you can relate to them in such a way that you facilitate their exploration and talking about the advantages and disadvantages of coming out and assessing possible values to be gained over against the risks of loss, then you have performed an act of mercy in the name of Christ.

We of course need to take account of the differences between teenagers coming out to their families and those who are young adult and sometimes approaching middle age, established in their work, having at least a few long-term sources of support, and probably by this time a number of close gay friends. The objective risk is usually considerably greater for the teenager who has established fewer external support systems. But the deep longing to be accepted by one's parent(s), sibling(s), and other family to whom one has feelings of affection and appreciation is very powerful for most gays and lesbians of any age. These observations of mine correspond with studies that indicate that relatively few teenagers clearly come out to their parents and therefore would not be talking with a minister about doing so in the same terms that an adult would. The teenager who does speak with a pastor would be more likely to raise the issue of confusion about sexual feelings and feel terrified about the possibility of his or her parents' knowing, with parents being drawn in only if professional counseling for fee is needed.

A study of various events in the life of gays and lesbians shows that the average age of coming out to parents is thirty for lesbians and twenty-eight for gay males.[24] The youngest to speak with me was a twenty-one-year-old woman who had already, in fact, just told her family and needed help to continue the process of explanation and reconciliation. I have also spoken to several men ages twenty-three to twenty-five and a few ages twenty-eight to thirty. Those who may come to you as a pastor usually do so not because they have no one else to talk to (although teenagers don't ordinarily have the options of persons to talk to that adults have, including that of professional therapists). But for a number of gays and lesbians, as well as for other people, there is something special about the pastor, the representative of God and the church. You might be their or their family's pastor, but you're not like other counselors. There is more risk in revealing themselves to you, although they somehow see that the gains might be greater.

"Pastor, I want to tell you something very important about who I am. I am gay (lesbian)." There may follow a discussion of their anxiety in talking with you, trying to come to terms with who they are sexually, and the stress of living a life of cover-up. They may long for a sense of God's love. They may reveal their sense of distance from those they love (family, long-time friends, and so forth). They want to look at the possibility of coming out to their family, people at work and at church, and other persons in other situations. One thing is sure: you can't give the person *the* answer concerning whether to come out to those named. The risks are quite real. There can be professional penalties. One or both parents may ban a child from the home; parents may agree, or a serious split between the parents may occur; a brother or sister whose friendship and support have been valued may withdraw; a good friend may be lost; the person may be shunned in church. *The minister does not know the answer.* But she or he may be a facilitator of a thorough exploration of the issues and engage with the person in a discussion of a strategy that would have the greatest likelihood of being effective.

Usually with the family, and perhaps with other significant groups, the initial strategy would consider identifying the one person who is most likely to respond with understanding and/or affirmation of love and support. This person, if responding positively, becomes an ally in telling the next person or persons in the family or other group. Very frequently the first person in the family to be told is the brother or sister to whom the person feels closest. If one or more family members or others to whom the gay or lesbian has chosen to reveal himself or herself have been quite negative, and sometimes they are, the minister can be a continuing refuge for the person in his or her pain, distress, and anger. Then together they may discuss the possibility of additional strategies, both in order to provide necessary support in this difficult time and also in regard to redeveloping relationships with family members and/or others over a longer period of time.

But remember at every stage of the process, never say, "If I were you, I'd. . . ." You can't *possibly* know what it's like to be that person. Never say, "You ought. . . (or ought not . . .)." Only the gay or lesbian person will take the consequences, so only that person should make the decision. The pastor is simply to assist in considering all possibilities.

In those instances where the response to the person is clearly positive, or gives indication that family, friends, colleagues, and others are willing to work at moving in a positive direction, there is usually a deep sense of relief and joy and new life for the lesbian or gay person. To come out to significant persons is not just a need to have a relationship of genuineness with them, but also a sense of genuineness within one's own self. Since many gays and lesbians have internalized society's stigmatization of homosexuality, they may tend to diminish their own sense of worth and have important areas of self-mistrust. They are fragmented and need to be made whole and have a sense of self-worth. "Coming out becomes a process of reclaiming disowned or devalued parts of the self, and developing an identity into which one's sexuality is well-integrated."[25]

We need to keep in mind, however, that even though the process often has this effect, few who are thinking about coming out are really aware of the possibility of this internal outcome, and it is seldom the conscious motivation. The motivation, as already mentioned, is the desire for honest relationship, relief from the strains of a life of secrecy, and often the outgrowth of some crisis related to their being gay or lesbian. But for whatever reason, growth in self-esteem, self-confidence, and a realistic sense of assurance may often occur.

Coming out to at least a few people in the work setting is also often seen as important. A number of lesbians and gays choose a particular setting for their work where lesbians and gays are already prominent;

thus there is no fearful pressure in coming out. In most work settings, however, this is not the case, and the need to have at least one person at work with whom one can be one's true self is very important. It is rare that homosexual persons have chosen to come out to a church congregation, Sunday School class, or young adult fellowship, except, of course, in congregations whose membership is predominantly gay or lesbian or in those congregations that, as a result of courageous, sensitive, and patient cultivation by a pastor, have openly decided to welcome lesbians and gays, including couples. (See chapter 6.)

Numerous gays and lesbians have had experiences that lead to the conclusion that coming out to family, some friends, co-workers, and others in groups that are significant to the person is worth the risk and even some number of rejections in order to achieve the personal growth referred to earlier, to receive affirmation for who one really is, and to lift the burden of secrecy. Yet, as has been said before, this is not to deny that in some cases there are some real losses and some long-term pain.

Coming out is not an easy decision, nor is it a simple process for most to go through. There certainly can be some unease, risk, and hard work for a pastor who may be counseling the person facing this decision and process. But it can be a rewarding one, regardless of the outcome, for the sensitive, skilled, caring pastor and her or his self-giving and service in the name of Christ.

THE COUNSELING OF COUPLES

Panic! *Two* lesbians or gays come to see us or call and ask us to visit them. Actually, there's no reason at all to double the anxiety we may have if it were only one. All we have to do is remember what we have learned about couple counseling in other situations. Of course, for most of us, any couple or family counseling situation *is* more difficult than dealing with only one person at a time, but as we read and study the process more and gain more experience in doing it, we can work with gay couples and lesbian couples just as effectively as we do other couples, although a number of their issues may well be different.

Let's face it. Most pastors are not actually trained in counseling two or more people at the same time. However, we can learn a few basic principles and strategies of responding. The fundamental task is to help each person express her or his feelings and needs and desires directly to the other, not to the counselor. The pastor then makes sure that the other person responds directly to what was expressed. Then the second person is encouraged to express his or her feelings, needs, and desires to the first, with the pastor assisting the first to respond directly to these. The pastor's task is to keep the focus on the present relationship between the two, listen to what each is expressing, observe how the other responds, and call attention to what is taking place between them. At times we may respond empathetically to one or the other and by doing so model the type of understanding they need to have and express to one another. As in individual counseling we ask each of them in turn to clarify the meaning of what he or she has said, occasionally stating our own feelings that have been aroused by something that has been going on. In so doing, we not only facilitate their communication with each other at the moment, but once again provide a model of communication appropriate for their relationship.

The process is to help them not only express themselves clearly in this moment and to respond to the other's expression, but we are also helping them to learn to be able to do spontaneously that which will improve their communication with each other outside of the counseling session, thus improving their relationship (or perhaps discovering that they cannot have a long-term close relationship as a couple). Communication of this sort will reduce the number of occasions for misunderstanding and conflict, yet when such misunderstanding and conflict do arise, the couple's problem-solving will be more effective.

This process can be used with any two persons if they desire to work something out between them. To be sure, some of the specific issues and problems presented may be related in some way to their sexual orientation, but their *relationship* needs and the pastor's helping process are the same.

Lesbian couples and gay couples usually seek counseling for just about the same reasons that any couple might. They would call upon a pastor, not usually because they believe that he or she would be more effective than a highly trained marriage therapist, but because the pastor represents the community of faith. In all honesty, relatively few pastors will be called upon to counsel with gay or lesbian couples. Usually such pastors will be serving a parish that is open to receiving gays and lesbians fully into the life of the congregation, and thus one or both in the couple already know the pastor in this context.

If the couple is previously unknown to the pastor, it is important to raise the question, as I do with all couples, married or unmarried (and individuals also), "How is it that you made the decision to come to me as a pastor rather than to some other counselor?" Frequently, though not always, this opens up a discussion of their own faith in God or their searching for faith and their own past or present relationship with a local church. Therefore, right from the beginning the context is set for all the other issues that they want or need to discuss. Like heterosexual couples, they may have discovered some rough spots in their relationship and want to see if they can learn to work these out satisfactorily. There may have been an emotional blowup and they're afraid to talk much with each other without someone else's assistance. Their relationship of love may have developed to the point where they're considering living together but would like to have the pastor help them evaluate the possibilities of their making a permanent commitment to each other, including the meaning of fidel-ity, agreeing to such a meaning, and pledging to abide by it. Those who have made such a commitment may then want further conversations that are like those we call premarital counseling. Marshall emphasizes, "Connecting spirituality and sexuality in the context of relationships remains one of the most profound gifts pastoral representatives can bring to their vocations,"[26] especially in the counseling of couples who are considering life commitment to one another.

This raises another issue for a number of clergy who take the position that it is not wrong or sinful for a person to *be* homosexual, who can understand and support a couple living together, but who believe that the Bible, Christian tradition, and ethical considerations prohibit sexual relationships between two people of the same sex under any circumstances. This is the position of Hays, a very reputable scholar, although as I follow the development of his interpretation of relevant passages of Scripture and other sources, I don't find the connection between what he says about the Scripture (and these other considerations) and his conclusion that gays and lesbians who take their Christian commitment seriously, "should seek to live lives of disciplined sexual abstinence."[27] Although I disagree with him, I find his reasons for such a position considerably better grounded in Christian thought than any others I have seen.

But what if you as a pastor agree with him? You're talking with a gay couple or lesbian couple who are in the process of committing themselves to one another for life. You certainly have every right, even the responsibility, to present as best you can your support for their relationship only if as Christians they live a life of "disciplined sexual abstinence," giving both of them the opportunity to ask questions and respond to your reasoning. You then invite them to think about this particular commitment seriously and prayerfully.

If they freely make such a decision in response to what they believe to be God's will for their lives, we can only ask God to bless them in this way of living out their faith. But what if, in response to the process of consideration in which you've led them, they say in some form, "No thanks" to the abstinent life, what will you do then? Obviously I can't tell you what to do, but let me simply ask, would it be possible for you to give a blessing (not necessarily to perform a ceremony of holy union) to their committed, faithful relationship with one another in which they choose to give sexual expression to their love, and can you then support them in their life together? If as a matter of conscience you cannot do this, and/or if church law prohibits helping them prepare for such a service and/or your officiating at it, it seems to me that the most pastoral act at this point might be to refer them to a minister who feels free to work with them toward such union. (See chapter 6 for Thornburg's excellent discussion of this situation.)

As a couple is seriously considering a service of covenant or holy union, it is essential, if the couple themselves don't initiate it, that the pastor raise the importance of the strongest possible social support for their life together. You will remember that one of Gaiser's criteria for marriage and for the union of lesbians and gays is "public accountability" (p. 63). But public accountability itself can be initiated by whatever social support can be mustered for the service of union. Therefore, in addition to gay and lesbian friends, the pastor leads the couple, if necessary, into a consideration of straight friends and members of the couples' families of origin. Some may cringe at the idea of inviting their families. Yet in a number of families there are some if not all who know that the person is gay or lesbian and who already are accepting and supporting. There may also be those whom the two persons need to think about coming out to, seek to gain support from, and then invite to the ceremony.

As in other issues in pastoral counseling, it's not useful to try to force people to do things, no matter how subtle you may be. (There are a few exceptions to this in some circumstances of extremity, such as suicide.) But also don't allow the couple to brush aside this idea of needing support of family and friends. If the couple can be integrated into the life of the church, so much the better. If the couple doesn't already know someone, the minister might invite certain trusted members.

Once a couple's commitment to one another has been made and they are living together, either with or without a service of covenant, there is a plethora of problems that any people living together may have: interacting with one's own and the partner's family (frequently with more varied and intense reactions than those of heterosexual couples); how the couple plans to handle the conflicts that arise; assignment of household chores; handling of finances; disagreements as to how neat to keep the house (or, how much chaos each one can tolerate); abuse of drugs (prescription or nonprescription, legal or illegal, including the drug alcohol); work schedules; reaching agreeable decisions when one has the opportunity of job change or promotion that means moving to another city; whether to adopt a child; problems in parenting an adopted child or one's natural child or children; how to face the situation in which one or both may be HIV-positive; differences or disagreements about religious practices and church attendance. Whatever situations heterosexual couples can get into, whatever problems they need to resolve, whatever relationship issues they need to discuss, lesbian and gay couples face also, frequently enough intensified by families' and society's prejudicial responses to them.

EPILOGUE

If your beliefs and feelings are such that you can't and/or don't want to counsel with gay or lesbian individuals and couples, what is a Christian pastoral response? What we *must* keep uppermost in our minds is that God loves us and God loves them and that we represent to them the God of love revealed in Jesus the Christ. We need to remember that we are called to be pastors (as well as preachers, administrators, educators, and so forth).

It seems to me that it would not be in line with the *pastoral* role to speak a condemnatory word or in any way convey a condemnatory attitude, even though your beliefs and feelings might in fact be disapproving. I believe that it's in line with the calling of a Christian to be able to help in ways within the range of our abilities to *anyone* in need. Any pastor would need to know the resources of his or her community and be able to make an appropriate referral. There may be other local church pastors who can work with gays and lesbians in ways we cannot. Professional pastoral counselors certified by the American Association of Pastoral Counselors are in every large city and a large percentage of small cities in the country. Many of these are accessible to persons who live in small towns and rural areas in no more driving time than it takes to drive to a pastoral counseling center in a large city. When there are critical issues such as depression, suicidal feelings, abusive relationships, or drug abuse (including alcohol), there are professional psychotherapists who are sensitive to issues of faith and specialized organizations such as Alcoholics Anonymous, Suicide Prevention Centers, other organizations, agencies, and treatment centers to which to refer or take people.

5

PASTORAL CARE AND COUNSELING OF FAMILIES OF GAYS AND LESBIANS

The last few decades have increasingly seen the family as it has been traditionally defined as an endangered species. This is not the place to attempt to name and analyze the forces at work to produce family tensions, conflicts, and breakdown, but merely to recognize it. Youth and young adult cultures are quite different from those of their parents.

A young adult woman comes home for a visit from college or from her work in another location and brings with her a male friend. The parents discover for the first time that the couple have been living together for months.

The parents in a family respected by the community inadvertently find a stash of drugs in their teenage son's bedroom, leading to their additional discovery that he's been taking them to middle school every day and selling them.

A twenty-year-old son comes home from college for a Christmas vacation. During the time at home, he tells his mother, or perhaps both parents, that he is gay. They are stunned. This can't be.

A clergyman of many years of successful ministry comes home for lunch one day, an unusual occurrence. The children are at school. He tells his wife that he is gay and describes the stress he has been under as a husband, father, and minister. He tells his wife that he loves her very much and wants an open and honest relationship with her. He also wants to be free to be with other men for love and sex. He would prefer to remain married, but he is willing to consent to divorce if that's what she wants. She is stunned and angry and says that of course she's going to divorce him. She herself has been fully aware of her sexual dissatisfaction for years, with sexual relations taking place only a few times a year with a very unenthusiastic partner.

These family scenes are being repeated daily, yet in much of contemporary discussion, the families of gays and lesbians have been the almost forgotten people, with only a relatively few books specifically for them. There are a number of groups and programs with a focus on the needs of lesbians and gays, but rarely groups for their families, an exception being Parents and Friends of Lesbians and Gays (P-FLAG).[1] However, some denominations and even local churches are beginning to form them. Many major Christian denominations have formal statements of their positions with regard to homosexual persons. Usually they acknowledge that gays and lesbians are loved by God and should receive the ministry of the church, even though such ministry seldom takes place self-consciously. But to my knowledge, none of these statements explicitly mention the special needs of family members of homosexual persons and the obligation and opportunity of the church to offer pastoral care to these families.

Family members of gays and lesbians are periodically involved in situations that cry out for a loving, sensitive, caring, knowledgeable pastor and congregation. Family members need a powerful reminder of the presence of God who loves them as this love is communicated in relationship with a congregation and a pastor who can be of genuine assistance to all family members in dealing with their own emotional reactions, facilitate clear communication between them, work in problem solving, and patiently lead them toward reconciliation.

COMING OUT IN FAMILIES

This topic has been discussed in the previous chapter from the point of view of the gay person. This section discusses briefly the situation and points of view of families. There are different ways in which the information that a family member is gay or lesbian becomes known. Frequently, within a family of several persons, there have been a sufficient number of hints and clues, rumors from outside the family, and evasions in conversations with one another that one or more of the family begin to suspect, then feel fairly certain, and sometimes know that the person is lesbian or gay. This may take place even without an open statement of it. Many parents, though, have an enormous capacity for denial of anything unpleasant to them when it has to do with their children, no matter how old the children are. Therefore it may be that brothers and sisters of the gay or lesbian person may be the ones who gradually make the discovery, but parents, exposed to the same situation, will still not be aware of it.

Lesbian and gay persons are caught in a trap and are usually tortured from each side of their dilemma. Almost universally they deeply desire an open and honest relationship with their parents and siblings or with their spouses. Yet they are usually very afraid of the family members' reactions: what they will think, feel, or do. These fears are not totally unrealistic, of course. Often enough there are very negative reactions, although the first reactions don't necessarily predict the long-term outcome. But it is this desire for an open and honest relationship in which they can be accepted and loved for who they are that leads to the direct coming out. Unfortunately, occasionally the family may hear such a revelation as an act of anger in the midst of a conflict. In this case, the working out of the relationship they desire has been complicated and intensified by the way in which the secret has come out.

If one of a married couple is lesbian or gay, she or he almost always tells the spouse first, rarely the children. Even here there are some exceptions, however, if a child is an older teenager or an adult with whom the parent has a good relationship and whose response the parent trusts. When the coming out takes place with the parents, it is often with the mother alone. There seems to be in most instances more uncertainty about how the father will react, more fear of what he may do, and the expectation of a more loving response and, even if not accepting, at least a less violent reaction from the mother. I have, however, been involved in situations where it is the mother who is unyielding and unforgiving.

However, for the well-being of family life, it is important in almost all occasions that eventually all of the relevant family members be told and that they all be involved in discussions. Telling only a sibling, while useful, will not bring the gay or lesbian person the degree of relief in feeling more a part of the family. Telling only one parent tends to produce a collusion between that parent and the daughter or son to keep their secret from the other parent. Such a collusion is disruptive to the family life and widens the emotional and trust gap between the parents themselves.

This very brief review of coming out is given because it suggests a strategy for pastoral counseling, as does the section that follows.

TYPICAL REACTIONS OF PARENTS

This section is titled as it is simply because I've had only a few instances of being involved with married couples in which one of them has discovered that the partner is gay or lesbian, and thus I cannot speak of spouses' typical patterns of response. I am aware that shock and denial are often present. Anger is extremely common. There is a sense of being betrayed. Often the spouse *has* been betrayed, sometimes by the gay or lesbian partner's knowing prior to marriage that he or she was homosexual, and often enough by the fact that the gay or lesbian partner has had sexual affairs during the marriage. I also am aware of instances where there is self-blame or self-depreciation by non-gay/lesbian partners. "It's because I wasn't a good enough sexual partner with him. I didn't want to do all the things he wanted." Or, "I'm not really a *man* if I can't make her love me rather than another woman." There is bewilderment. "What are we going to tell the kids?" "I can't bear letting anyone else know about this. I'm humiliated. What am I going to do?" The anger may take the form of "There's no way I'm going to let him [or her] have the children. I don't even want them to see him [or her] any longer."

A well-known physician, after over thirty-five years of marriage, told his wife that he was gay. Interestingly, she had seen me as her pastoral counselor quite some number of years before, speaking of her dissatisfaction with their sex life, or more accurately, their lack of sex life. Her husband just wasn't interested. So now the husband's revelation was not a total surprise. They did divorce, but they did so as friends and remained friends.

Again, let me say, my knowledge isn't sufficient for me to see a detailed and consistent pattern.

Of course, parents and other family members differ considerably from one another and no family is exactly the same as another family. Therefore everyone does not respond exactly like the general pattern I am going to present now. Many Christians have especially difficult reactions because of the fact that their Christian faith is vital to them, the Bible is God's self-revelation to them, and they believe that sexual acts between people of the same sex are condemned by the Bible, which means by God.

Dr. Jimmy Allen, a prominent Southern Baptist minister, recounts his struggle. He speaks of the clues he noticed after his son Skip's graduation from high school: things his other two sons would say and Skip's discomfort in his dating relationships with young women. Later Skip and a young woman became engaged, but it broke off suddenly. Finally, Dr. Allen asked him directly.

"Skip . . . didn't blink. He answered matter-of-factly, 'Dad, I'm gay. God made me that way, and I can't do anything about it.'"[2]

Allen describes his reaction as being like a blow to the stomach from a boxer. With all the clues, he still had not dealt with the real possibility. But there was the reality, "challenging me, almost taunting me. . . ." He goes on:

As one who takes the Bible seriously as the authority for life, there was no way I could justify homosexual behavior. Gently, but firmly, I reminded Skip of some of the Scripture passages regarding the subject. He was not convinced. . . .

After Skip's departure, the reality of the situation ripped into my heart and mind with unremitting vengeance. I felt instant stomach-wrenching remorse.

One of the first reactions . . . was to ask myself, *What had I done as a father to make this happen? Good kids didn't change their sexual preference overnight, especially good kids that have been raised in a Christian home. Surely I must have failed Skip somehow. His homosexuality must be my fault. But how?*[3]

The agony of a Bible-believing Christian pastor and father!

Later he declared: "There are elements of my son's lifestyle that I do not understand and cannot condone. On the other hand, my son is much more than his sexuality. And I love my son."[4]

A young man told his mother that he was gay. Her response was a reaffirmation of her love and support. But together they decided that there was no reason to tell the father about it. The mother had some questions about herself, some internal discomfort, both of which were resolved in just three counseling sessions. However, the whole family was not united. The father remained excluded.

With most parents, however, there are a number of rather common responses that can be arranged in stages somewhat chronological in the order of their occurrence and are, in fact, the stages of grief.[5] I hope that an understanding of these stages and some of their behaviors will give some clues to pastors as they are involved with the family.

Shock and Denial

A middle-aged couple were referred to me by a psychiatrist who was the therapist for their thirty-year-old son who lived and worked in another city. During the young man's early twenties, after a great deal of confusion, conflict, and guilt for several years, he finally came to the conclusion that he was gay and that he was going to have to accept it. His fighting against it, coming as it did out of his own conservative Christian home and the almost universal expectation that everyone was heterosexual, biased him against himself. He had gone to the psychiatrist to seek help in continuing to come to terms with himself as a gay man, clarify some of the relational problems with a fairly new love partner, and to see what he could do in talking about who he was with his parents, who at this time thought that he was someone else. He finally told them that he was gay. Their immediate response was, "No you're not. You couldn't be. We didn't raise you that way." They encouraged him to return to the church and the faith of his childhood and youth. When he tried to explain to them that this was not something he just decided, but was essentially who he was sexually, they simply couldn't understand it.

These were well-educated and very intelligent people. They were active church members and deeply committed Christians. But their minds simply could not handle the reality that their son loved men rather than women. They didn't understand. Therefore it was more acceptable to them to think of him as defiant. That was something that could be worked with. His being gay was not. Contrary to their way of thinking of him at this time, what he really wanted was an honest and loving relationship with them. But their denial would not allow it. Especially shocking to them was hearing him say not only that he *couldn't* change, but that he *didn't want* to change. He had already gone through all the usual ways of trying to get rid of his sexual feelings for males, his guilt, and his self-doubt by praying and by seeing a psychiatrist. Over a few years he adjusted to the reality of who he was and now he felt fine about himself. The parents simply could not believe it.

This is not the only situation in which I have known parents who refused to hear and believe what their child said about being gay or lesbian. The radical change in their lives, the disruption of their dreams, and for most, the terrible pain of it usually produce a reaction of shock, a sense of unreality, or no feeling. Occasionally there may be intense anger, which also can be a way of denying the other feelings the parent may be experiencing.

Yearning

As the shock wears off, as the denial breaks down in the face of reality, or as the intensity of anger diminishes, most parents move into a period lasting a few weeks to perhaps many months. The experiences of this stage are related to the parents' sense of the loss of the son or daughter that they thought they had. That child has died or gone away. They catch themselves looking at the daughter or son, or hearing them on the phone, and think "that looks and sounds just like him [or her], but it's not really the same person." Their dreams and expectations, both conscious and unconscious, have been destroyed. In the minds of all of us, the dreams and expectations of a loved person, the one whom we would like for the person to be and thus believe the person to be, become merged with who that person really is. So with the loss of many if not most of those dreams and illusions, it *feels as if* the person whom they knew was dead. The parents are grieving in ways similar to grief in a loss by death. The difference is that the person is still alive and we have to do something with them.

The word "yearning" refers to this aching longing for what *was* (as the parents perceived it). They seek in their minds to reproduce the past, remembering their child in many stages of his or her earlier development, often crying as they do so. They remember their dreams of what the future with their child would have been like: working, marrying, having children and one big happy family; not having the pain and stress they are now realistically experiencing.

Anger may arise in this stage if it had not before, or in a form that it had not been felt before, often accompanied by blaming: blaming their child for "doing this to them"; blaming his or her friends for influencing their child, luring their child into this different (and bad, sinful) life. They feel the pangs of guilt as they blame themselves, searching their own lives for what they did and didn't do that might have influenced their child to turn from the "normal" direction of development. "If we'd only let him play school sports like he wanted to." "If we only hadn't let her play with those rough boys for so many years when she was little." "If I'd only been at home more, done more things with her (or him)." "If we only hadn't argued so much in front of her (or him)." The searching can be endless, but it is ultimately fruitless.

The yearning produces behaviors in which the parents attempt to get the son or daughter to change back like she or he was. Threats are attempted, but they fail to do anything except widen the gap. Bribes are offered but not received.

I've been involved with a family in which the father, though active in the church, three or four times a year would leave home for several days with two or three other men friends of his to go to a large city and spend the time drinking, gambling, and picking up prostitutes. When his grown son told the family that he was gay, the man couldn't stand it. He was so concerned about his son's terrible sin. He copied passages in the Bible dealing with homosexual acts and mailed them to the son with the plea that he read them prayerfully and ask God to change his life (that is, sexual orientation).

Another young man's mother was trying to use the Bible to entice him to change that which he could not change by bombarding him with various quotations from the Bible. He said to me, "In all of my life, I've never known my mother to be interested in the Bible before."

Anything to make it like it was, like we hoped it would be. I hope that you don't think that I'm caricaturing parents in these excerpts. They are serious and pained, and I am just as serious as I can be in describing their reactions. They hurt terribly. They are anxious. They feel helpless. Some feel desperate.

Putting all of what's been said in describing this stage together, it presents a rather drastic picture. But much of it describes what some parents go through, and some responses describe most parents.

Transition

This stage is characterized by a diminishing of the intensity of most or all of the feelings that parents have experienced; letting go of their dreams; attempting to see their son or daughter and themselves more realistically; trying to learn more about homosexuality and what they're experiencing; perhaps seeing a minister or another counselor if they've not already done so; beginning to give up trying to change their child's sexual orientation. Parents feel somewhat better. They're not so preoccupied with their child. But they still have periods of sadness, a longing for what they thought the child was and would become, but this is less consuming for them. It's really impossible to generalize about how long this may take. For some, it will be only a few weeks or months. For others, tragically, it may never end.

Resolution-Reconciliation

Unfortunately, as I have just suggested, this stage is not always reached. For some parents, their final stage is the failure of the transitional stage to be a transition, and therefore they are stuck with their feelings of sadness, incompleteness, pain, disillusionment with their child, etc. There may be an uneasy truce, with conflicting feelings within each parent; between husband and wife; with the daughter or son. In extreme, some begin the adjustment to complete or almost complete separation from their child.

But many parents do come to an acceptance of the reality of their child's sexual orientation. They may feel entirely all right about it, or they may still feel some longing and sorrow at times. But they've passed beyond anger, blaming themselves and others, no longer feeling guilty, no longer accusing their daughter or son.

The highest quality of this resolution comes when there is a genuine reconciliation between the parents and between the parents and their son or daughter. This reconciliation is clearly possible and is a source of joy when it is experienced. This should always be the goal toward which a pastor should attempt to lead the persons involved. Reconciliation is a relationship in which the persons accept and love one another as they are; are honest with one another, even when not always approving of all attitudes and behavior; forgive easily and fully; and enjoy one another.

Of course, there are often siblings. Reference to them has been omitted from this discussion of the stages, because their inclusion adds so many variables that the attempt to describe them all would be impossible. Yet the active involvement of the siblings is usually more useful both to the parents and to the gay or lesbian than it is neutral or complicating.

THE PASTORAL CARE OF FAMILIES OF GAYS AND LESBIANS

First, how does a pastor become involved? It's not at all like a family member's calling and saying, "John has died. We'd like for you to come see us." Or a church member's calling and saying, "I heard that Mrs. Reeves went to the hospital today. I know it would mean a lot to her if you'd go see her." Pastors get these calls, if not every day, certainly every week. But how often do we pick up the phone and the person on the line says, "I've just heard that Susan's family has found out that Susan's a lesbian." These calls are extremely rare. In fact, I've never gotten them. If you do hear this about Susan's family, are you *expected* to go visit them? You want to be of service, but what service? There are opportunities, but there are also dangers. What if Susan *is* lesbian, but the parents *don't* know? What if Susan is not a lesbian? Either way, the parents very likely don't want the pastor to call. Yet we also need to be alert to helping whenever we can.

This is not a situation where people flood pastors' offices. Families are usually reluctant. A number of parents who desire to talk with a pastor about their son or daughter do not go to their own. I've heard things such as:

"He just wouldn't understand."

"He's a good preacher, but he seems so rigid."

"She's just so liberal she'd only take our son's [daughter's] side against us."

"We're very active in that church, and we're afraid of what our pastor would think of us."

If the parents go to any professional, they are likely to go first to a psychotherapist, who may then refer the parent(s) to their minister or to a pastor other than their own. Parents' fears need to be understood and appreciated. There is no room for jealousy because *my* parishioners have gone to another pastor to talk about their homosexual child and their reactions to their finding it out. If members of another congregation come to you, what's your responsibility? A pastor's responsibility is to be of service to them in the name of Christ. This would always include the question as to whether they had already gone to their own pastor. If they have, and have been rebuffed in any way, then proceed to work with them. If they have not, I believe that it's our responsibility to help them explore the reasons they made the decision to come to someone else first. If up to this point they have been satisfied with their own congregation, they need to reconsider whether it might be more valuable to them both now and in the long run to talk with their own pastor. But we must do this in such a way that we do not communicate that we are rejecting them. After reconsideration, they're free to make their own decision.

This is clearly a sensitive situation for clergy: to what extent and under what circumstances might we serve *temporarily* as pastors to members of another congregation? We certainly need to act ethically with regard to other clergy, yet we need to be as certain as possible that people are able to be in a relationship where their needs can be met. If the family members persist in their desire to talk with you, then you need to be very clear that you are willing to do so only until this situation is either resolved or reaches a point where you can no longer be helpful. We must also be very careful not to be a temporary pastor to people in such a way that we are also seducing them to become members of our congregation. Of course, if for any reason we believe that we cannot play a constructive pastoral role with these people or in this type of situation (or any other, of course) we need to be candid with people about that and refer them to a pastoral counselor not serving a local church.

Perhaps the more frequent situation is when the lesbian or gay person has made the first contact with the pastor. Whether this comes originally by that person's initiative or whether the person has been talking with another counselor who recommended it, the person is raising the questions of whether to tell the family, how to tell the family, when to tell the family, and is perhaps asking the pastor to be present at the time of telling. On other occasions the lesbian or gay person is concerned about one or both parents' pained, confused, sometimes angry response after they have been told or have found out in some way about the sexual orientation of their child. Unless there are compelling reasons to the contrary, the pastor could suggest that the gay or lesbian person tell the parents about the visit to the pastor, clarifying that you would very much like to see the family members as a whole group to discuss their reactions.

If the gay or lesbian person calls back in a few days indicating that some members of the family would come and that others would not, then invite those who are willing to do so. If the pastor does not hear from anyone within a few days, it would be appropriate to call the gay or lesbian person to see if he or she has talked with family members. If not, it would be useful to discuss the reasons that this has not taken place. If after the gay or lesbian person has talked with the family and no one seems to be willing to come for this conversation, you as the pastor are well within your rights, with the permission of the lesbian or gay person, to call the home, talk with one or both of the parents, and indicate that their son or daughter has come to see you, and that you are aware that their child has asked them to be in touch with you. You could suggest to the parent(s) the extreme importance of their participating in some conversation about their situation with someone. Invite them to come to your study, express your willingness to come to their home, or if they prefer, refer them to some other pastor or professional counselor. It does seem to me that it would be useful to point out that their daughter or son is wanting to have a good relationship with them and that from that person's point of view there really is a great deal to talk about. Actually, I have found it rather rare that no one at all in the family would respond to the invitation.

Meeting with the Family

Just as rare as it is that no one participates following a request from the lesbian or gay family member and/or pastor, it is equally rare that an entire family will participate in the first session, desirable as that might be. We talk with those who come and attempt to work toward the enlisting of the others to participate.

Keep in mind that the primary goal is reconciliation. Parents usually at first think of this as reconciliation between the homosexual child and themselves, with their first responses indicating that the terms are that the child must change. Even though no two people within one family always react to their gay or lesbian family member the same way, there is sometimes a well-developed expectation that everyone within that family think and feel the same. Married couples often have that expectation of each other and certainly expect children to follow suit. Naturally this leads to some difficulties. Therefore the process of reconciliation between all family members can be quite complicated.

For the most part, especially early in the conversation, the pastor's role is simply to facilitate communication between each family member and the others. Each person in the family is encouraged to say what she or he is thinking or feeling at this time. It is also very important to discover the feelings that underlie each person's beliefs. Then check with others to see if they have understood. Don't just ask the question, "Does everyone understand?" Ask someone to paraphrase what his or her understanding is. Check this understanding with the others. *Without understanding there will never be reconciliation.* We need to keep in mind that it is just as important for the gay or lesbian person to understand each parent and other family members as it is for them to understand him or her. Can the lesbian or gay child understand the parents' shock, anger, blame, guilt, and attempts to get her or him to change? Can a husband and wife understand and respect the differences between themselves and differences between the children and themselves? Is there a family member, often a brother or sister, who can be active in helping people understand one another? If so, this person becomes an ally with the pastor in accomplishing what needs to be done.

From time to time the pastor may summarize what she or he understands has been said and checks that out with the family with regard to its accuracy. Periodically the pastor will also probably need to ask what a person means by what he or she has just said in order that everyone understands the same thing.

The pastor's function is to be a facilitator of expression on the part of every family member about the family situation in which they are all involved and assist their communication with each other, leading, one hopes, to increased understanding among them all.

Remember that this first time together is not an occasion for arguing about what the Bible says, assessing blame, making threats, or arguing with each other about any point. The pastor must be sufficiently assertive to intervene and remind anyone who begins to move away from the goal of the expression of feelings and responding to one another that the purpose of this first conversation is the developing of mutual understanding. Some pastors as well have to be careful to restrain themselves at this point and not prematurely express her or his own views about homosexuality, the Bible, church pronouncements, etc. In addition, if in the first session a family member were to ask about the biblical pronouncements concerning homosexual acts, or begin a statement, "Well, the Bible says . . . ," the minister needs to resist taking the bait.

Rather, she or he must remind the family of the overarching importance of continuing to work on understanding one another. Assure them that there will be time to discuss the Bible and any other issues thoroughly at a later time.

If the self-expression has gone well, if people have been able to understand that other family members feel a certain way, if they can appreciate (not necessarily agree with) the other person's perspective, if intensity of feeling has diminished, this has been a very important accomplishment for the family. With some number of families this process will move along very well and progress will be made, even though differences of belief and feeling are still there. With others, the pastor will have considerably more trouble. Why? The answer is simple.

Levels of family functioning. Families begin with a man and woman with different needs (both conscious and unconscious) and behaviors that are designed (mainly unconsciously) to meet these needs. They may have different views of what a marriage and what a family should be, learned in their own families of origin. Each is led to establish a relationship with a life partner to some large extent on the basis of their perception of how the other is meeting his or her needs. They have children who inevitably learn in infancy, childhood, and adolescence to behave in certain ways to have their significant needs met by these parents (or parent, if one is now out of the family and thus out of the picture). (See the discussion concerning us clergy, pp. 66–67.)

There are obviously different levels of family functioning that tend to reproduce themselves from generation to generation. What I've described so far is not that everything is absolutely determined by these families of origin, but there is a strong tendency toward attempting to maintain the meeting of one's own needs in a way first learned in one's own family of origin. It is crucial for the pastor to be able to recognize the roles people play in their families and what the typical patterns of behavior are (especially how they communicate) in order to attempt to adjust her or his own methods of working with a particular family.

Three levels of family functioning have been identified in the Timberlawn Healthy Family Study. These three levels also have higher, medium, and lower levels of functioning within each one of them.[6]

The *healthy family* is characterized by adaptability, flexibility, relatively little authoritarianism, and respect for the others' points of view and the differences between them. Communication is open and free-flowing, with emotions being expressed openly and accepted by the others. The level of empathy is high. This type of family will be responsive to the pastor's leading them in conversation about a family member's being gay or lesbian and their reactions to that information. At some point in the conversation, after all have had the opportunity to express themselves, it can be effective to present alternative methods of interpreting the Scripture and to discuss some of the information about possible sources of homosexuality.

The *mid-range family* gives the appearance of unity and may truly love one another, but upon examination the unity is mixed with the requirement of sameness. Parents expect and require sameness of opinion and feeling of one another, and they expect that of their children. Guilt is a predominant feeling. Opinions are evaluated in terms of right or wrong: little ambiguity, little in-between, always this or that. Rigidity is a major characteristic. Parental authoritarianism dominates. The pastor faces a number of difficulties in working with them. Her or his major support will be whatever love they have for one another.

You may expect that it is difficult for them to change habitual behavior and to change their opinions, but it is not impossible for them to come to an acceptance of reality and allow their genuine love to appear and encompass their child. For me, although not necessarily for all, in addition to seeing the whole family together, it may be more effective to see members of the family individually and in pairs selected for their compatibility. We hope that various ones will then have a positive influence on the others when we have the family together for a conversation. We always need to be careful that we never contribute to an irrevocable split between the married couple. The purpose in pastoral counseling with a mid-range family is not to attempt to change their overall basic pattern of functioning, because most of us are simply not capable of that length, intensity, and complexity of family therapy. We seek to discover and use the strengths that they do have in the service of their accepting the reality that a family member is gay or lesbian, diminishing the intensity of their initial feelings, and nourishing their love for one another.

The third level of family functioning is that of the *severely dysfunctional family*. It is doubtful that a pastor will ever be effective in pastoral counseling with these families as a whole, although we can often be of service to various family individuals. Their family pattern is best characterized by the word *chaos*. There is very little consistent family structure. People speak at the same time, interrupting one another. A group session can be bedlam for all but the most experienced psychotherapist. Individuals tend not to take responsibility for their own behavior; there is a lot of blaming of others, inside and outside the family. They speak for others more than they do for themselves. Each believes that he or she knows what the other people are thinking, so words and actions with each other are often inappropriate.

The pastor who is not assertive and confident in that situation is doomed to confusion, anxiety, and failure with this family. To me, the best rule of thumb is to talk individually with family members. Assess the needs of each as best you can. At some point it is important to talk with the parents as a couple. You may well need to refer them to a pastoral counselor or other psychotherapist who is trained in family therapy.

Practical procedures. After a first session with family members, regardless of the family's level of functioning and regardless of what the pastor has been able to accomplish with them, a second session is very important, even though you've seen some of them as individuals. Very few if any families complete the understanding and reconciling process as a result of just one conversation. Often people do not want to come back. Their resistance to continuing can take many forms, most of which pastors are already familiar with:

"Thank you so much. You've been so helpful. I (we) think that every-thing's all right now." Counter with your own observations that led you to recommend that they have another session.

"We'll see. We'll think about it and give you a call," (followed by no call). The pastor is well within her or his rights to call them after a reason-able period of time.

There can be others; just keep your emotional ears tuned. Remember, things may have been tough on the pastor in this session, too, triggered by the amount of overt anger, conflict between persons, intense sadness, or lack of cooperation by some. But the people usually *need* to talk fur-ther. So check around with every person with regard to his or her will-ingness to meet again. If some want to and some don't, help them talk with each other about it and attempt to get the family consensus. This may issue in the pastor's having individual and/or couple conversation with family members.

A second family group meeting session might very well begin with a review of each person's reflections on what took place in the first group ses-sion and their feelings at this point and a discussion of any conversations they've had with each other. If two people have talked together but haven't shared it with the whole family, this would be the time to do it. Clarifica-tion of any misunderstandings that remain between any of the persons needs to be dealt with. Differences in belief among them can be discussed more fully and clearly as the intensity of feelings is reduced. Some of the family may have questions to which the pastor may now respond directly.

If the parents happen to say that God and/or the Bible condemns homosexuality or homosexuals, the pastor, regardless of his or her inter-pretation of the relevant biblical passages, can go ahead at this point and clarify that the Bible is not speaking of the sexual *orientation* of what we call homosexuality and that it is the behavior that is condemned. Regardless of the clarity of the Bible about this, many people have gotten the wrong idea into their heads. This is not a big step, but it is one of some significance to some number of people.

But remember the goal, *reconciliation within the family,* including the lesbian or gay person, regardless of who believes what. The pastor needs to be alert to and even search for clues that might assist in distinguishing between those family members of genuine Christian faith and who take the Bible seriously at *all* times and those people, even some church members, who are really not devout and who are now simply using the Bible as pressure on the gay or lesbian family member. Strategy with each will be different.

For most families a major barrier is the belief that the gay or lesbian person could change his or her condition or could enter into some process whereby he or she could change. With such a change, the person could then move along with the usual parental expectations of heterosexual marriage, children, and so forth, while at the same time saving the family from shame, disgrace, scandal, or embarrassment. For many families it is helpful if they can accept their family member's own experience for what it is, a sexual orientation, that cannot be changed. This assumes that the gay or lesbian family member is not an early or mid-teenager or perhaps somewhat older but still having some of the characteristics of teenagers—uncertainty about his or her sexual identity and inadequate experience in establishing friendships and dating those of the other sex. In these instances it only makes sense for the young person to see a competent and unbiased professional counselor for a period of time. I recognize, however, that this is impossible for many people, and others have a strong resistance to doing this.

Regardless of their own beliefs, conscientious pastors can always let people know about available information and point them to reading that might help them understand their own reactions and assist them in talking through the issues.[7] Gay and lesbian persons themselves can often be helped in understanding their parents' reactions. Such information might even be discussed in this or later sessions.

By this time, either the parents have stated explicitly that this experience feels like the loss of their child and recognized that their behaviors are those of grieving, or if they have not done so, the pastor gathers together what they have stated at different times and suggests to them the similarities of their experience with grief. This recognition supplies a framework for understanding their sense of helplessness, their complex and conflicting feelings. Often anger is the result of the loss itself, with the lost but still-present one being accused as the one responsible for their loss.

If family members can genuinely understand their own reactions as grieving, it provides the pastor the opportunity to summarize briefly what may lie ahead of them in terms of the stages and the behaviors and experiences within each stage. The pastor can point out that there may be several occasions over the next few months when they might have the need to talk with him or her again: when they get discouraged, when they consider how long it's taking to reach some stage of peace or satisfaction, when strong feelings recur, or other troubling reactions arise. The married couple alone may need to talk with a pastor now or later with regard to how this new situation in the family has affected their relationship.

If the parents (or another family member) have raised the issue of what the Bible says about homosexuality, homosexual persons, or homosexual acts, this second session is often a time when the subject can be addressed in detail and the issue as to whether the gay or lesbian person can or cannot change can be discussed. The pastor has to judge whether the intensity of emotional reaction, especially on the part of the parents, has subsided to the point where factual material and cognitive discussion can be listened to and evaluated. Intellectual presentation cannot be heard or evaluated on its own merits by the person who is totally under the sway of his or her strong emotions. Sometimes such a discussion of scientific research, varying interpretations, and so forth may need to come even later than the second session.

The gay or lesbian person can in this session recount (again and in greater detail) what her or his experience was as she or he first became aware of feelings of attraction to persons of the same sex. As a group, gay and lesbian persons have had different individual experiences, and yet there is a core of sameness to the majority of them. They can tell parents and other family members of their struggles, their not wanting this for themselves, measures they have taken in order to change, all to no avail, their surrender to what they have seen as inevitable for themselves, and finally their acceptance of it at whatever level they are at the moment. The pastor's role is to be a guide to the gay or lesbian person through this story, perhaps by asking questions that would lead to greater detail, or by asking members of the family what they understand about the story at different points. The pastor ought not to lose track of her or his explicitly being an emotional support to the family members during this session.

The family may now be ready to talk about the Bible. The pastor, regardless of his or her interpretation of the relevant biblical passages, can remind them, if it has not been stated earlier, that the Bible is not speaking of the sexual *condition*, just the sexual acts. Pastors, of course, are not helped by English versions of the Bible that use the word "homosexual(s)" or "sodomite(s)" in 1 Corinthians 6:9 and 1 Timothy 1:10, so that will take some explaining. (See pp. 42–43 and later discussions in chapter 3.) The next step might be to help the family understand that the Bible was condemning homosexual acts under the circumstances in which such acts were known at the time and that homosexual relationships of love and commitment, especially between adults, were not known to the writers at that time. This discussion, of course, stops short of what many people, including a number of clergy, believe about homosexual acts being wrong under any circumstances. If the minister can do so conscientiously, she or he might lead the family into a consideration of the approach taken in chapter 3, although with whatever differences the pastor may have with that material.

If the family and/or the minister still believe that the biblical references are to all homosexual acts, even in the situation where people have committed relationships of love with one another, there is no need to continue with a discussion of the Bible's explicit references. But remember that the goal is not ultimately *forcing* people's beliefs (even your own) but reconciliation within the family. Regardless of what the Bible says about many human behaviors, can a family be united in love and mutual support? Can a pastor serve them lovingly to meet their most important needs right at this time? If parents take the Scripture quite seriously for themselves, the pastor might focus their attention on the goal of their group meeting by pointing to Scriptures such as 2 Corinthians 5:18: "All this is from God, who through Christ reconciled us to himself and gave us the ministry of reconciliation."

For those whose interest in the Bible has been aroused only by the news that their child or other family member is lesbian or gay may be introduced not only to 2 Corinthians 5:18 but to other similar passages as well. However, in the instance of family member(s) concerned only with the homosexual passages, they can be led to understand the feelings that have stimulated their flight to the Bible, getting these feelings out in the open where they can be responded to.

During this session, the gay and lesbian persons themselves can be helped in understanding their parents' reactions and thus the overall level of tension reduced. We have to remember, however, that even when the pastor has used all of her or his knowledge, sensitivities, and skills, full reconciliation does not always come about.

I continue the story begun on pages 118–119 about the parents who responded to their thirty-year-old son that he couldn't be gay because they were people of faith and had raised him in the church. They had interpreted his stating that he couldn't change simply as defiance. Because of his "defiance" they banned him from their home and after a period of time removed him from their will. They could not emotionally tolerate this "different" person who "claimed" to be their son. The young man was deeply hurt and angry. He longed for a good relationship with them. It was this disruption of the relationship that had led the psychiatrist to suggest the parents talk with me.

Naturally the parents were also deeply hurt and angry, uncomprehending. How could their son do this? It was in violation of the Scripture, the teachings of their church, and the standards of their family. They believed deeply that if he would only repent and nurture his faith, he would not any longer want to do what he was doing. They loved their son, but until he came around to their point of view, he would no longer be allowed in their home and would remain disinherited.

The third and last session we had was one of the most heartbreaking experiences I had in forty-four years of full-time ministry, and there have been many. The primary goal of the young man, whom I saw only once, and of the parents, was reconciliation. The primary task in the first two sessions with the parents was to help them with their sense of loss of their son as they had known him, their deep pain, and their feeling somehow that their son was consciously rebelling against them and punishing them by his being gay. I noted the differences between the reactions of the married couple themselves as we discussed the passages in the Bible, also giving them some information about homosexuality as a condition. Together we tried to clarify what they wanted to see happen: reconciliation. But the parents set the firm conditions with no alternatives. Their son must change. He must give up this "idea" that he was gay. *Then* they would be reconciled. We discussed their feelings at length. Their son had tried to change, and it had not worked. But they were adamant, and they restated their demand of him.

I then asked, "But what if he doesn't change?"

The father made all of the responses; the mother was absolutely silent and expressionless: "Then he can't come back. We have no relationship."

"But you said that you really love your son."

"Yes." Tears came into the father's eyes and trickled down his cheeks. "I love him so much." And he began to sob. A long pause—"He's sinning."

"But what if he absolutely can't help being who he tells you he is? Can that be sin?"

No answer.

I continue: "What if he absolutely *cannot* change?"

"Then he can't come back into our house. We can't see him."

"But it sounds as if you're very unhappy not seeing him."

"Yes."

My voice is getting softer and softer as we go along, and I am becoming sadder and sadder myself and more and more frustrated: "But if you were to believe that he *can't* change, couldn't you change your minds and invite him back?"

A long pause.

The father in a very low voice: "It's too late," and he wept.

Tears trickled down my cheeks also. The mother was dry-eyed, impassive.

I feel that sadness even now as I write these words many years later. We ended the third session shortly thereafter, and I never saw them again.

There have been numerous more successful conversations with others and happier endings than this, but I simply recount this incident so that we might be realistic about the occasional extreme difficulties that we might have.

I can think of no better way to conclude this section than by reference to a recent official message from the American Roman Catholic Bishops in which they reemphasize in the teaching of their *Catechism* that homosexual persons "must be accepted with respect, compassion, and sensitivity." Speaking to the parents of gays and lesbians, the new pronouncement "notes that parents need to accept themselves and their own struggle; to accept and love their child; and to accept God's revelation about human dignity and sexuality. . . ." In a clear and helpful statement they say, "Your child may need you and the family more than ever. He or she is still the same person. This child, who has always been God's gift to you, may now be the cause of another gift: your family becoming more honest, respectful, and supportive."[8]

WHEN THE GAY FAMILY MEMBER HAS AIDS

When a man tells any family member that he is gay, it is inevitable in these days that the family member wonders if he has AIDS. The reality of AIDS in the world today is an unavoidable issue, adding an unspeakably powerful sense of horror to a revelation that to parents especially is bad enough in itself. Unless the man has already told his family member or members his HIV status (negative or positive; if positive, any further relevant information), it would be important for the concerned family members to ask, because wondering is just as complicating to what they're experiencing as knowing. The knowledge of his being gay and the reality or possibility of his infection complicates their reactions. Parents and/or a spouse are trying to sort out their feelings and deal with their distress. However, family members often do not ask because they don't want to know, because they don't want to offend their son or spouse, or for other reasons.

If a pastor is involved, he or she needs to be sure that the family knows what being HIV-positive is and what having AIDS is. It is also crucial to family life that they know the very few circumstances of the transmission of HIV; the only major concern for almost all families is taking care that the blood of the infected person does not get into an open wound of a family member. They do not have to "be careful" about the usual acts of family living: hugging and kissing, eating with the same utensils, using the same bathtub and toilet seat, etc.

Family members need to be encouraged to talk openly about their fears. Some of these can be dealt with effectively simply with information. Others can't, and especially if the gay person has begun to have symptoms of AIDS, there are going to be some very sad and stressful times, with the probability of death at some point. In these instances the pastor functions as she or he would when a family has any one of several other diseases that has a long and complicated course. The family can get very tired, at times exhausted, with a person who is bedridden with AIDS; they can become hopeful when the disease seems to be dormant, only to be plunged quickly into the horrors of the reappearance of symptoms that demonstrate its worsening. At the same time, early on, the pastor needs to be working with the family on the issue of the son being gay. It is a very difficult time for all involved.

From time to time anger at the gay man may arise because "he did this to himself (and to us), and I am so furious with him because of it." This is natural, and clergy can expect it, just as they do in families when a member drank too much and drove and had a serious accident and is badly injured or even was killed. It takes place when a family member severely abused his or her body through overwork, use of drugs, inadequate rest, smoking too much and becoming ill, then perhaps refusing to go to the doctor, and sometimes dying of this self-inflicted disorder.

People may, in this as in other situations, express their own feelings and confusion by age-old Jobian questions: "Why has God done this to us?" "Why does God allow there to be such a disease?" or by statements like, "He's being punished for his sin." Clergy need to be the world's experts in responding to these and similar questions and statements and to the feelings that lie behind the questions by giving direct information when it is available and at times the profound answer, "I don't know." Yet we can always go on, "But I *do* know that God loves you and him with a powerful love." Different responses to different people at different times. Be sensitive to the needs that these expressions reflect and respond directly to the needs, not necessarily first to the theological implications. People are not inviting a theological lecture at a time of deep distress. Rather,

"I know it's difficult to understand why such suffering exists," or ". . . why you have to be experiencing such anguish."

"It's making you wonder about God's love."

"It sounds as if you're really angry at God about all of this."

We need to sort out the types of responses that communicate some understanding of what they're going through and that enable them to speak further about their experience.

If the gay man is not HIV-positive, another immediate issue of concern to parents, and to the pastor as well, is the gay man's sexual lifestyle. More and more gays have a regular love partner, sometimes a life commitment to sexual fidelity to the person, though sometimes not. If they are in such a relationship, they may offer the information. If the information is not offered, I personally believe that it is proper to ask. If they do not have a special friend, more than likely they are engaging in sexual relations at least from time to time, though sometimes not, just like many single heterosexual men. They may be having frequent anonymous sex. All of this, of course, relates to varying degrees of probability of their becoming infected with HIV, a concern for everyone involved.

If the pastor is invited into the family situation because the parents have discovered that their son is gay and at that time or later reveals that he is HIV-positive or even is beginning to have symptoms of AIDS, then the pastor knows that he or she is probably going to be in touch with the family immediately and then off and on over a long period of time. They will have different needs at different times. As I have already stated, if the time of infection is very recent, it may be several or many years before symptoms of AIDS appear, if they do at all. The pastor's first action is to check in detail on the needs of the family as they may be entering the first stage of anticipatory grief and also have some individual conversations with the son who is HIV-positive or has AIDS.

If the son is not seeing a physician, we can recommend one or more physicians who specialize in the treatment of HIV-positive persons and PWAs. It is crucial that we know the community resources that are in all metropolitan areas, most small cities, and sometimes in rural areas for the purpose of meeting whatever needs the family and the PWAs have: support groups for parents and for PWAs; homes for those debilitated with AIDS and whose families can't handle their housing; home health care nurses, companion or buddy programs for the PWA. Look in the business pages of the phone book under AIDS, call the county health department, or when a person is dying, call a hospice program.

If a period of time passes without our hearing from the family or the PWA after the first several conversations, it is not only appropriate but essential that we call or go by to see them. Go, be at ease, shake hands, hug, have a cup of coffee or a soft drink if it is offered. I would not have thought it was necessary to say this until I read the following excerpt from Allen's book:

> One of the most disappointing reactions came from one of our pastoral friends. When he heard that Brian [their infant grandchild] had passed away, the pastor came to visit our family to offer his condolences. I was not at home, so he stayed and spoke briefly with Wanda [Mrs. Allen].
>
> In the course of their conversation, the pastor politely asked, "What was the matter with the baby?"
>
> "He had AIDS," Wanda answered matter-of-factly.
>
> The pastor stood to his feet, and almost as a reflex action, his hands flew up in the air as if he were trying to stop traffic. "Oh, oh, oh!" he said, as he backed away. The pastor quickly concluded his visit and left our home without even shaking Wanda's hand. . . . [I]t did not escape us that

the first pastor who had an opportunity to minister to our family as victims of AIDS failed to reach past his fear. With some members of my family he never got another chance.[9]

There is nothing to fear. Being frequently in touch with the parents and their son is a necessary and meaningful ministry.

The Funeral of the Person with AIDS

To me, the funeral is always a worship service of the church, a concern of the congregation. Many of the participants fairly often don't see it that way, but my design and the one I suggest is that it contain all of the elements of a worship service, although they need not be in the standard Sunday morning form. Only if the family states compelling reasons to have a service in another way might we after thorough discussion with them do something else if our conscience allows us.

To say that the funeral is a worship service means to me that there should be a sermon. This does not exclude eulogy, but eulogy may come in different forms. My usual approach is to include many references to the person as illustrative of points in the sermon. An intimate knowledge of the person is invaluable. We do not always have that sort of knowledge directly, but we can always be sure that we make time to talk at length to the family and hopefully with a number of friends of the person. A family member may want to give a eulogy, or they may want to ask another person to do so. For me, that is fine, but it does not replace a sermon, and the eulogy would always be presented before the sermon.

After the death and before the funeral it is essential always to talk with as many of the whole family who can come together at one time. The pastor should encourage every person present to speak openly and freely about the family member who died and their feelings now after his death. If necessary, help the family accept differences of opinions and feelings and work to help everyone understand and accept one another. This process is effective pastoral care of the bereaved as it facilitates their being supportive of one another. In addition, for the pastor, it is helpful preparation for the funeral.

An occasional controversial issue is whether the deceased's life mate, life partner, partner in love, faithful friend (all these are terms taken from obituaries I have read) is to be present as a family member for the pre-funeral conference and whether he will sit with the family at the funeral. Some family members have rejected the mate from the beginning and would not let him in their home. This is a genuine tragedy. It is the same as rejecting their own son. The fact is, from their son's perspective, this mate is as fully a part of the family as any daughter-in-law or son-in-law could be. Often the life partner has been faithful in ministering to their son throughout his illness, sometimes with a larger investment of time, money, and emotional energy than some of the original family members. He deserves to be there.

We can and should tell the family ahead of time that we believe that it would be useful for him to be present. It will give some of them the opportunity to express their misgivings about him; perhaps some will express their appreciation for him in the presence of those who disapprove. Family members will have the chance to hear him tell of his love for their son and how he had cared for his partner during the illness and share some of his good memories. The family may even come to know not only the mate but also their son better.

I have a vivid and meaningful memory of such a loving and candid session with a family immediately after one of the sons had just died of AIDS: the two parents, two daughters and the spouse of one, three sons and their spouses, and the committed lover of their son. There were a total of thirteen of us there. The session took almost two hours, but it was very moving and extremely valuable and helped me tremendously in preparing for the most meaningful funeral for the greatest number of people. Not all of the family members felt the same about their brother. Some were candid in expressing some of the difficulties they had had with him over the years. But everybody seemed to be united in love, and very good memories were shared with each other. Everyone agreed that AIDS should be openly referred to. The funeral service and the sermon were difficult enough for me to prepare for, since I had gotten to know the son very intimately while he was in the hospital and I had begun to care for him very deeply. The session with the family helped me emotionally as well as giving me relevant material for the sermon.

An issue for some pastors and some families is whether in the funeral to talk openly about AIDS or not. I definitely prefer that freedom myself, in the sense that I don't have to make cautious preparation. In addition I believe that to be able to have the reality out in front of us in the service contributes to the healing of the family and others and allows the pastor to make comments that will be helpful to all present. Some members of some families are reluctant. The pastor will need to present his or her point of view to them as sensitively and convincingly as possible.

A compelling illustration of the need for honesty is recounted by Dr. Allen. Lydia (the daughter-in-law) finally died of AIDS, which she contracted through a blood transfusion. The family was together at the funeral.

> During the ceremony, Scott [Dr. Allen's son and Lydia's husband] and Matt [Scott and Lydia's little son] were by my side. I could feel Scott's anger rising as he sat rigidly through the songs, eulogies, and prayers. After the service, Scott got up and left the church without a word to anyone. Before doing so, he said to me in a terse, quiet voice, "Nobody said the word AIDS in the whole service."[10]

Almost everyone in the church knew that Lydia had died of AIDS. But no one said it.

Only if the family members closest to the one who dies insist that AIDS not be mentioned, even after hearing the pastor's reasons for openness, should the pastor follow their wishes.

CONCLUSION

In the pastoral care of families, especially that which extends over a period of time and where there is intense need, it is easy for us pastors to lose our focus. The individuals' needs often differ. There are different opinions in the family about homosexuality and different reactions to the gay or lesbian family member. Parents especially want their child to be like she or he *was* (that is, the way the family *thought* the person was), thus putting the pressure on the person to "change" in order to be a full-fledged family member. There can be conflict. At the same time the lesbian or gay person, in her or his frustration, needs for the *parents* to change, to accept her or him like she or he is. AIDS complicates the family picture significantly. Different ones make different pleas to the minister, and their needs are more urgent in the face of impending sickness, growing gradually worse, and ultimately leading to death.

If the pastor gives in to all of the pressures on him or her to do everything that everyone seems to need, he or she may have several possible reactions. One is simply to withdraw from the situation, partly consciously, partly unconsciously. Less and less attention is given to the family. Most of the pastoral care is only to this or that individual. Finally the pastor becomes busy with other matters and may withdraw entirely. Another is to try to please everyone, getting confused by all that is going on and feeling as if he or she is not at all sure what needs to be done or how he or she can do it. Confusion and despair set in, and if any pastoral care is attempted at all, it is relatively ineffective.

Therefore, it is always crucial for pastors to remain focused on the goals of pastoral care: to live out the compassion of Christ in as effective a way as possible with particular people in particular situations. With a family, even though attention is given to individual needs, caring is ultimately more effectively done by focusing as often as possible on their relationships with each other. Pastoral care of families seeks to elicit the expression of thoughts and feelings and identification of needs with one another within the family. It tries to help people listen to one another more carefully. The goal is to facilitate understanding and to stimulate mutual acceptance, even when family members may not accept one another's opinions or behavior. All of this often leads to uncovering their love for one another.

A final goal is to bring about reconciliation within the family, because reconciliation is the will of God. The pastor needs always to be conscious of the fact that he or she is the representative of the community of faith, a symbol of the love of God, and a constant reminder to the family and each individual that God is in the midst of the process. This may be reinforced within the process by particular words of the pastor, by clarification of the Scripture, and by prayer. The proper pastoral care context in working with the family struggling to understand one another when a family member is gay or lesbian or struggling mightily with their own feelings when a family member has AIDS, is the reality that all of us stand constantly in need of the grace of God. The pastor represents the grace of God by his or her own gracious relationships with the people involved.

6

THE CONGREGATION AS A CARING COMMUNITY FOR GAY MEN AND LESBIANS

by John Thornburg, Pastor
Northaven United Methodist Church, Dallas, Texas

It was Mother's Day. Those who planned worship had chosen a set of prayer petitions to help members of the congregation express both joy and lament.

> *For our mothers, who have given us life and love, that we may show them reverence and love, we pray to the Lord.*

There was a chorus of names. Some of the voices were filled with emotion.

> *For women, though without children of their own, who like mothers have nurtured and cared for us, we pray to the Lord.*

The chorus continued. There were tears in some eyes.

> *For mothers, who have been unable to be a source of strength, who have not responded to their children and have not sustained their families, we pray to the Lord.*

When this last petition was read, three different women turned in their seats and gently placed their hands on the hand of a young man seated close by. After the service, that man sought out one of the pastors because this prayer had evoked the depth of his pain. Some months before, strengthened at least in part by the fact that he had a church family that affirmed him both as a child of God and as a gay man, he had come out to his parents. They severed ties with him immediately and took such actions as returning the Christmas gifts he sent them without opening them. He needed his pastor to hear the pain of his continued separation from his mother.

This chapter is about being the kind of congregation in which this man could *receive* the care offered by the women around him and then *seek* additional care from either the clergy or the laity. This chapter is not primarily about pastoral care techniques, but rather about re-creating the way we approach being a caring community of faith and sharing the message of hope that such a re-created community has to offer. This chapter is also not about what straight folks can do for gay men and lesbians, as if care only goes in one direction. It is about the ways in which people in Christian community can receive multiple gifts of grace by being brave enough to challenge accepted myths about the church and about homosexuality.

139

OFFERING RADICAL HOSPITALITY

Being a re-created congregation must be rooted in an initial act of radical hospitality. Because very few congregations make it plain that gay men and lesbians are as welcome as anyone else, merely making an internal statement of the intention to be inclusive is not enough. It's one thing to have an open house. It's quite another to actually invite people to come to it.

Pastors must preach and clergy and laity alike must model a radical grace that illuminates the shameful practice of modified grace practiced in many communities of faith. Whether they truly intend to or not, many people of faith proclaim by their words and actions that some people receive the unmerited gift of God's grace without stipulation simply because they are the children of God, while others receive it *only if* they are willing to change and become heterosexuals. This amounts to creating different classes of people. One class receives grace, which makes new life possible. Another can only receive grace when they have come into compliance with societally accepted norms for ethical behavior.

We must have the courage to say that this double standard related to God's grace makes common sense blush. Grace is not earned. If it were, it would not be grace. What has happened in most congregations is that we've played the disgraceful game of creating categories of sin and have proclaimed that gay men and lesbians are the "state of the art" sinners. In an odd way, we ought to take comfort in being one in sin, because, at the very least, it precludes the possibility of separation through judgment.

I think that many people are fearful that if they proclaim God's radical grace, they will be seen as condoning any and all behavior. It's essential to separate the act of proclaiming grace and welcome to a hurting world from the act of discerning and maintaining ethical standards in human community. Both are important, but they are different tasks. It is deeply legitimate to worry about cheapening grace by not paying any heed to the actual behavior of people. It is also essential not to condone forms of behavior that are abusive, hateful, dangerous, or promiscuous. But it is irresponsible to decide that every act and every thought of every gay man and lesbian is sinful *simply because he or she is gay*. If a congregation is to offer care to gay men and lesbians, that congregation must be unequivocally clear that they are welcome in the fullness of their being, including their sexuality, by virtue of the fact that they are children of God.

DEMONSTRATING THIS HOSPITALITY

Hospitality at the Door

It is important to spend intentional time with those who greet visitors (ushers and other greeters), dealing sensitively with their feelings and sharing the vision of inclusive community with them. If these people are fearful, gay visitors will know it immediately.

It is essential, when possible, for the pastor(s) prior to worship to circulate among the congregation meeting people and urging current members to meet the visitors. If gay men or lesbians (or a gay couple) visit, they may bring more than the usual sense of anxiety about entering a new congregation because they also bring the concern about whether they have to be secretive. Sensitive acts of hospitality help reduce the fear.

In the Language of Worship

Worship language can easily reflect the heterosexual experience, whether it is the formal language of liturgy or the informal language of the parish announcements. The most important linguistic stumbling block is the use of the term "family." Churches have code language, and one of the clearest forms of code language in the church is the use of the term "young family" to mean a family with a husband, wife, and some number of children. If we speak only about our need to have more "young families," it creates the picture that the only way a congregation can grow and be vital is with the addition of young, heterosexual couples with children.

Congregations can grow in any number of ways, including growth in families in which there is a single woman or man (with or without children) and in which there are two men or two women. Also, due to the tragic loss that many gay people feel if cut off from their families of origin, they often form groups that then function like families. These are often called "families of choice," as distinguished from families of origin. Communities of faith must cherish their role as a family of choice for many people with their own distinct forms of woundedness. Churches must be ready to receive and enjoy the gifts of many different kinds of families. In greeting new visitors, I often say, "Tell me about your family." I do so in the hope that it allows them to define family in their terms.

We must make it clear that all in the congregation have "access" to the congregational prayers, so that if a gay couple is celebrating an anniversary, they are encouraged to share their joy with the congregation. The congregation I serve offered a gift of grace a few years back when a gay member would offer prayers on a variety of subjects, some of which seemed to call on God to endorse Democratic politics. There were some rumblings in the congregation about whether it was appropriate to have "gay activism" creeping into our prayers. On more than one occasion, a thoughtful straight member of the congregation would break up the gossip by reminding a group that Democratic politics had been mixed into our prayers for years! Humor is sometimes the best cure for fear and anxiety.

In Preparation of New Members

While deeply aware that many churches do not have formal training or instruction for new members, I find this the single most important place to introduce my concern that we be a congregation that extends radical hospitality. Because we are in a denomination that prohibits the ordination of "self-avowed practicing" homosexuals, and because our denominational social principles state that "we do not condone the practice of homosexuality and consider it incompatible with Christian teaching," we must deal with the immense barrier that this presents to gay men and lesbians who are attracted to the mission and ministry of our congregation but are hard pressed to understand why their behavior is being judged even before it is observed.

Two things are immediately necessary. First, we can't ignore those official positions or pretend that they are insignificant. Adopting the attitude "it's not as bad as it seems" won't work. It's like pretending that the deutero-Pauline injunctions to women to be subject to their husbands and to be silent in church "aren't as bad as they seem." The much more honest thing to do with people who are preparing for membership is to give them an accurate account of the relevant denominational history (the good and the bad) and an account of the ups and downs experienced by our congregation as it wrestled with matters of inclusion. We have to be honest in enunciating the fact that most denominational positions are compromises that have been forged on the backs of gay people. We need to say that we are sad about that fact and find it deeply unjust. We need to say what we believe is wrong with our denominational positions, how we are working for change in them, and how people can join in that effort. Then we need to show the signs of hope within our denomination by telling the stories of individuals and congregations that are making a difference.

Second, it's essential to enunciate a vision. I say to my prospective members, gay and straight, that my vision is that some day when openly gay people enter the church, they will simply be known by the name everyone else has: child of God. I have a vision that straight couples with children will seek out a congregation like ours *because of* our inclusion, and not *in spite of it*. I have the vision that all straight people who visit and join will dismiss the stereotypes of gay men lurking around the restrooms for young boys precisely because they have met gay men and worked side by side with them in all matters related to the church.

Anything less honest than this will be seen as deceptive. Those who have been the objects of discrimination all their lives do not need the further insult of being dealt with dishonestly. When we are unwilling to be compassionate, we sometimes resort to courtesy. God save us if all we can be as a community of faith is courteous.

BEING ATTENTIVE AND CARING TO THOSE
WHO FEAR CHANGE

There is no way to become a church in which gay men and lesbians feel truly welcome without recognizing the need to be highly attentive to the fears straight people bring to being part of an inclusive congregation. Because so many straight people, and especially straight men, lack the experience of having a close friendship with an openly gay person, the church will continue to deal with people's fear of the unknown for some time to come. Some of the fears are:

- that gay people will be publicly affectionate with each other in distasteful ways
- that if too many gay people join the congregation, the church will become a "gay church"
- that straight individuals, couples, and families who visit will be discouraged from returning when they see the make-up of the congregation
- that a gay man or lesbian might do something inappropriate with a child or one of the youth
- that a gay man or lesbian might mistake the sexual orientation of onc of the members and "come on" to a heterosexual

These fears are legitimate. If the congregational ethos is friendly but reserved, then public displays of affection by *anyone* can be difficult. If most of the people joining the congregation are gay, then the vision of inclusive community is threatened. Even if we despair at society's general attitude toward gay men and lesbians, that is the attitude being brought into the congregation every Sunday by our visitors, and we have to deal with it. We *ought* to be concerned with a straight man or woman doing something inappropriate. And when we are already feeling a little vulnerable in a community, there is added vulnerability if we have to worry about someone being attracted to us, gay or straight.

When you put these fears together, they are actually symptomatic of a deeper and more pervasive fear in any congregation: the fear of change. If there are established patterns of leadership and established understandings of what the congregation "stands for," the influx of a new group of people is very threatening. When you add to that mix the fact that most of the new people are under forty, have a different worldview, and are not lifelong churchgoers, the threat intensifies. The fact that many are openly gay simply adds more "unknowns" into the mix.

Over the past several years, the congregation I serve has wrestled with the whole question of how public to be about our inclusiveness. A consensus was reached in the late 1980s that the church would make the offer of radical hospitality. That consensus, though hard to reach, was healthy and solid. More than that, the consensus was backed up by the concrete behavior of the congregation. There was no vocal bigotry, and people showed patience and compassion as they worked side by side. There were (and still are) miracles of grace that allow people to give up their fears and stereotypes and embrace a new gift of human community.

But having decided to "open the doors," the congregation then began to face the complex set of questions about what our responsibilities were as people of faith to share our own convictions about inclusive community beyond the church walls. It was one thing to have *internal conviction.* It was a whole different question to do *external witness.*

During one of the episodes in which we struggled most intensely with our public witness, there was a gathering of people almost all of whom opposed explicit forms of "going public." Most opposed joining our denomination's national organization of congregations that are open and affirming to gay men and lesbians. As we worked through people's feelings and concerns, my impression was that we were dealing as much with the fear of change as we were with homophobia. There was homophobia. That was undeniable. But many people expressed the fear that the congregation was becoming something very different from the church they had joined years before. The biggest plea I heard that night was "Don't leave us out."

There is an intersection of realities here. We have the reality that gay men and lesbians have a justifiable anxiety about entering a mainstream church. The church has been so brutal to gays that it is easy to understand why gay people have a fear that a church's friendly exterior may be accompanied down the road by a thorny interior. And we have the reality that churches, like almost all organizations, are filled with people who fear change.

I am convinced that there are three keys to standing with integrity at this intersection: honesty, communication, and humor. The congregation can be a caring community for gay men and lesbians only if everyone in the congregation is being addressed honestly and being allowed to speak. At least twice a year in our principal worship service, I reflect on what I hope we are doing to move to new places in our journey toward inclusiveness and how I think we are doing. What I am attempting to do is to take step two in the process of being honest, step one being the work I do in the membership preparation classes.

At these moments, humor is helpful. I'll say something like, "Wouldn't it be nice if our most important social concern was whether to use paper or foam cups for our coffee?" I am attempting to explicitly and publicly recognize that people are anxious, but that some forms of anxiety are worth having. I want to publicly recognize that even if we are struggling, we're struggling with something deeply important. I want to testify that God's gift to us is not just the end of our journey, but the journey itself.

In some ways, Jacob is our patron saint. If the pastor or a key lay leader speaks with this kind of candor, conversations throughout the congregation are sure to follow.

In the midst of wrestling with being a congregation of radical hospitality, it's important to remember that fear is a two-way street. If a straight man is worried about a gay man "coming on" to him, then the gay man is just as worried about inappropriate sexual overtures. Again, it's important to claim with honesty and humor that we all want to be in a place that is safe and healthy.

DECISIVE, BUT NOT IRRESPONSIBLE, ACTION IN RAISING UP LEADERS

If gay men and lesbians are received into membership in the church, then it is an insult and a waste not to name them as leaders and to allow the church to benefit from their energy, talent, and spiritual gifts. In too many churches, gay men and lesbians are given the message (usually implicitly, but sometimes explicitly) that they can worship and put their gifts in the offering plate, but if they expect to be named as leaders, they are mistaken.

This is a miscarriage of baptismal justice. The recognition of someone's baptism (a key part of what we do when people join the church) is meant to be a radical act. It means that they are part of the general ministry of all Christians. But if we then turn around and say that the general ministry of all *gay and lesbian* Christians is confined to worship attendance, tithing, and attendance at churchyard clean-up days, we've made a mockery of the baptismal vows.

At the same time, it is pastorally unwise to "clear the decks" of existing straight leadership just to make the point that gay people can be competent leaders. The greatest sense of trust between gay and straight people in the congregation will come from shared leadership of major responsibilities. Justice demands that *neither* gay nor straight members of the congregation be allowed to engage in segregation. People feel care when their talents are respected and employed. Likewise, they feel rejection and loss when their energy is ignored.

Small group interaction in study, prayer, and fellowship is a wonderful way to develop the trust needed to have gay and straight leaders serve side by side. A series of dinner groups and a dedicated commitment to open dialogue in our women's group were two of the ways that trust has been built.

CLARITY AND HONESTY IN ALL MATTERS

When I was appointed to the church I currently serve, I was aware that there were a number of openly gay people. I also knew that to that point in my life I did not have an openly gay person as a friend. That meant that I was nervous about the new relationships I was about to have. I questioned my ability to relate with ease and comfort. I worried that I would stumble and say stupid things.

I was also aware that I might be asked to preside at holy union ceremonies and would most certainly be asked my opinion on some of the controversial issues related to homosexuality. On the question of holy unions, I became aware of deeply conflicting feelings: the sense of calling to affirm covenantal love between two men or two women versus the fright of losing my orders or facing scorn from my peers.

I knew that I did not want to walk this path alone. So early in my ministry at this church, I invited a group of parishioners, gay and straight, to meet in the home of one of the church members. I had, at that point, been asked to preside at a holy union ceremony and was dealing with the full force of conflicting feelings.

I explained to the group that the order of the church was clear. Were I to preside, I would clearly and unequivocally be outside the order of the church and, because of that, the church hierarchy would have the authority to take my orders away. We expressed sorrow and some anger. We talked about the differences between working within the church for change versus working outside. We talked about the trade off of staying within a church that had a position we clearly thought was flawed theologically and grounded in fear versus the reality that the only way to fully express the depth of my conviction in safety was outside the church.

I had come to that meeting with the conviction that I must say no to those who came requesting my presence at their union ceremonies because of my prior conviction that the best way for me to be in ministry was to work for change within the system. Those who attended joined me in the conviction, though not without sorrow and disappointment.

The event taught me three things. First, it taught me that being a leader means being clear, but you don't have to (and often can't) discover that clarity all on your own. In order to be the leader of a caring congregation, I need to involve people at all levels in determining how best to be caring. Second, if decisions are to be made in the church about the welfare of gay men and lesbians, they ought to be at the table. It would be like forming an older adult council in the church but not having any older adults present. Third, when the order of the church places prohibitions on clergy behavior, then the best way to offer care to someone is to be absolutely honest and clear. If I had said to a couple who came requesting my presence at a holy union that I *couldn't* do it, that would have been false. The fact is that I could do it, and risk the possible consequences. What I need to say instead is that I *won't* preside at the ceremony, explain why that's true, and express the depth of my regret.

Being clear and being honest are essential no matter whom you're dealing with in the church. They are especially important in ministry to and with gay men and lesbians precisely because they have been told so many lies by society.

A JOY TOO DEEP FOR WORDS

Since stereotypes are demonic metaphors, each congregation has the task of being involved in the daily and weekly exorcism of those demons. What we seek to exorcise is the fear that what is different is evil or abnormal. The fruit of that exorcism is a different view of reality: a view that is not naive, but is more open to the rich gifts that people have if you have the compassion to look for them and the patience to listen to them. I am a much richer human being because of the gift of compassion I have received from the gay community. If compassion can be likened to light, and hatred and discrimination can be likened to a long dark tunnel, then it's important to say that in the midst of the good struggle to be an inclusive community of faith, a little light goes a long way.

NOTES

INTRODUCTION

1. Joseph Harry, "A Probability Sample of Gay Males," *Journal of Homosexuality* 19 (1990) 96.

2. Alfred C. Kinsey, W. B. Pomeroy, and C. E. Martin, *Sexual Behavior in the Human Male* (Philadelphia: Saunders, 1948).

3. Harry, "Probability," 92.

4. Ibid.

5. Ibid.

6. *U.S. Bureau of the Census Statistical Abstract of the United States: 1995,* 15th ed. (Washington, D.C.: 1996).

7. "After Good-bye—An AIDS Story." KERA-TV, Dallas, Texas, 1993.

8. Larry Kent Graham, *Discovering Images of God: Narratives of Care Among Lesbians and Gays* (Louisville: Westminster John Knox, 1997), 11.

9. David K. Switzer, *Parents of the Homosexual* (Philadelphia: Westminster, 1980), now extensively revised as *Coming Out as Parents: You and Your Homosexual Child* (Louisville: Westminster John Knox, 1996).

1. THE CONSTANT DILEMMAS OF PASTORAL CAREGIVING

1. David K. Switzer, "Now Who's Coming to Dinner? Pastoral Care for Family and Friends of Gay and Lesbian People," *Word and World,* 14/3 (1994) 259. Used by permission.

2. Larry Kent Graham, *Discovering Images of God: Narratives of Care Among Lesbians and Gays* (Louisville: Westminster John Knox, 1997), 4.

3. Howard Stone, *The Caring Church: A Guide for Lay Pastoral Care* (Minneapolis: Fortress, 1991).

2. WHAT IS HOMOSEXUALITY AND HOW DOES IT COME ABOUT?

1. John Boswell, *Christianity, Social Tolerance, and Homosexuality* (Chicago: University of Chicago Press, 1981), 49-50.

2. For a detailed discussion of pederasty and its cultural background, see Robin Scroggs, *The New Testament and Homosexuality* (Philadelphia: Fortress, 1983), chapters 2–4.

3. Arno Karlen, "Homosexuality in History," Judd Marmor, ed., *Homosexual Behavior: A Modern Reprisal* (New York: Basic Books, 1980), 78–79.

4. Bernard J. Bamberger, *The Torah: A Modern Commentary* (New York: Union of American Hebrew Congregations, 1981), 736.

5. William L. Petersen, "Can *Arsenokoitais* Be Translated by 'Homosexuals'?" *Vigilae Christianae* 40 (1986) 188.

6. *Oxford English Dictionary*, "Homosexuality" (Oxford: Clarendon, 1989).

7. For a compelling account of such a struggle by an evangelical Christian, see the autobiography of Mel White, *Stranger at the Gate: To Be Gay and Christian in America* (New York: Simon and Schuster, 1994).

8. Michael G. Shively and John P. DeCecco, "Components of Sexual Identity," Linda D. Garnets and Douglas C. Kimmel, eds., *Psychological Perspectives on Lesbian and Gay Male Experiences* (New York: Columbia, 1993), 81.

9. Garnets and Kimmel, *Psychological Perspectives,* 54.

10. Joretta L. Marshall, *Counseling Lesbian Partners.* (Louisville: Westminster John Knox, 1997), 17.

11. Ibid., 17–18.

12. Ibid., 19.

13. Sigmund Freud, "Three Contributions to the Theory of Sex" (1905), in *Basic Writings of Sigmund Freud* (New York: Random House, 1938), 554–59.

14. Ibid., 560–61.

15. Ernest Jones, *The Life and Work of Sigmund Freud,* vol. 3 (New York: Basic Books, 1957), 195.

16. J. Michael Bailey, and Richard C. Pillard, "A Genetic Study of Male Sexual Orientation," *Archives of General Psychiatry* 48 (1991) 1089–96.

17. Ibid., 1094.

18. Ibid.

19. J. Michael Bailey, Richard C. Pillard, Michael C. Neale, and Yvonne Agyei, "Heritability Factors Influence Sexual Orientation in Women," *Archives of General Psychiatry* 50 (1993) 217–23.

20. Ibid., 221.

21. Dean H. Hamer, Stella Hu, Victoria L. Magnusen, Nan Hu, Angela M. L. Pattatucci, "A Linkage Between DNA Markers on the X Chromosome and Male Sexual Orientation," *Science* 261 (1993) 321–27.

22. Simon LeVay, "The Difference in Hypothalamic Structure Between Heterosexual and Homosexual Men," *Science* 253 (1991) 1034.

23. Lee Ellis and M. Ashley Ames, "Neurohormonal Functioning and Sexual Functioning: A Theory of Homosexuality and Heterosexuality," *Psychological Bulletin* 101 (1987) 235.

24. Susan Golombok and Fiona Tasker, "Do Parents Influence the Sexual Orientation of Their Children? Findings from a Longitudinal Study of Lesbian Families," *Developmental Psychology* 32 (1996) 3–11.

25. Ibid., 8.

26. Ibid., 9.

27. Ibid.

28. Ellis and Ames, "Neurohormonal Functioning," 235.

29. William Byne and Bruce Parsons, "Human Sexual Orientation," *Archives of General Psychiatry* 50 (1993) 236.

30. Ibid., 237.

31. Bailey, et al., "Heritability Factors," 223.

32. John Money, "Gender-Transposition Theory and Homosexual Genesis," *Journal of Sex and Marital Therapy* 10 (1984) 75.

33. Philip W. Blumstein and Pepper Schwartz, "Bisexuality: Some Social Psychological Issues," in Garnets and Kimmel, *Psychological Perspectives,* 169.

34. Ibid., 171–82.

35. Wayne Dynes, "Bisexuality," *Encyclopedia of Homosexuality,* Wayne Dynes, ed. (New York: Garland, 1990), 146.

3. WHAT THE BIBLE SAYS ABOUT HOMOSEXUALITY
(HOMOSEXUAL ACTS)

1. Albert C. Outler, ed., *John Wesley* (New York: Oxford University Press, 1964), 93.

2. Victor Paul Furnish, *The Moral Teaching of Paul: Selected Issues,* rev. ed. (Nashville: Abingdon, 1985), 68.

3. John Boswell, *Christianity, Social Tolerance, and Homosexuality* (Chicago: University of Chicago Press, 1981), 94.

4. Derrick S. Bailey, *Homosexuality and the Western Christian Tradition* (London: Longmans, Green, and Co., 1955), 2–3.

5. Boswell, *Christianity,* 94.

6. N. Oswalt, "The Old Testament and Homosexuality," Charles W. Keysor, ed., *What You Should Know About Homosexuality* (Grand Rapids: Zondervan, 1979), 73.

7. W. Gunter Plaut, *The Torah, a Modern Commentary* (New York: The University of Hebrew Congregations, 1983) 129–30.

8. Ibid., 130.

9. Victor Paul Furnish, "The Bible and Homosexuality: Reading the Texts in Context," Jeffrey S. Siker, ed., *Homosexuality in the Church:*

Both Sides of the Debate (Louisville: Westminster/John Knox, 1994), 20. Citing Richard Bauckam in "Jude, Second Peter," in *Word Bible Commentary* (Dallas: Word Books, 1983), 54.

10. Richard B. Hays, "Awaiting the Redemption of Our Bodies: The Witness of Scripture Concerning Homosexuality," in Siker, ed., *Homosexuality in the Church*, 5.

11. Bernard J. Bamberger, *The Torah: A Modern Commentary* (New York: Union of American Hebrew Congregations, 1981), 877–78.

12. Ibid., 878.

13. Ibid., 887.

14. Oswalt, "The Old Testament and Homosexuality," 56.

15. Ibid., 58.

16. Ibid.

17. Ibid., 59.

18. Bamberger, *The Torah*, 877–78.

19. Robin Scroggs, *The New Testament and Homosexuality* (Philadelphia: Fortress, 1983), 101–9.

20. Ibid., 29–65.

21. Ibid., 29.

22. Ibid., 35.

23. Ibid., 41.

24. Ibid., 42, 62–63, 108.

25. Ibid., 107. See also Arnold J. Hultgren, "Being Faithful to the Scriptures: Romans 1:26-27 as a Case in Point," *Word and World* 14/3 (1994) 317.

26. Scroggs, *New Testament and Homosexuality*, 83.

27. Ibid., 107–8.

28. Ibid., 109.

29. Furnish, *Teachings*, 72.

30. Alfred, Marshall, trans. *The Interlinear Greek-English New Testament* (Grand Rapids: Zondervan, 1978).

31. Scroggs, *New Testament and Homosexuality*, 120.

32. Hays, "Awaiting," 8.

33. Furnish, "The Bible," 26; *Teachings*, 65–67.

34. Scroggs, *New Testament and Homosexuality*, 114–15.

35. Ibid., 116.

36. Frederick J. Gaiser, "A New Word on Homosexuality? Isaiah 56:1-8 as a Case Study," *Word and World* 14/3 (1994) 280–93.

37. Ibid., 283.

38. Ibid., 287.

39. Ibid., 288.

40. Oswalt, "The Old Testament and Homosexuality," 52.

41. J. Harold Greenlee, "The New Testament and Homosexuality," in Keysor, *What You Should Know*, 106.

42. Ibid., 108; Oswalt, "Old Testament and Homosexuality," 75; John W. Drakeford, *A Christian View of Homosexuality* (Nashville: Broadman, 1977).

43. Hays, "Awaiting," 14–16.

44. Gaiser, "A New Word," 291.

45. Ibid., 292.

4. PASTORAL CARE AND COUNSELING OF GAYS AND LESBIANS

1. B. R. Simon Rosser, "A Scientific Understanding of Sexual Orientation for Pastoral Ministry," *Word and World* 14 (Summer 1994) 257.

2. Conrad Weiser, *Healers: Harmed and Harmful* (Minneapolis: Fortress, 1994), 3.

3. Lorna M. Hochstein, "What Pastoral Psychotherapists Need to Know About Lesbians and Gay Men in the 1990s," *Journal of Pastoral Care* 50 (Spring 1996) 76.

4. Ibid., 77.

5. Earl D. Wilson, *Counseling and Homosexuality* (Waco, Tex.: Word Books, 1988), 52.

6. Ibid., 51.

7. Larry Kent Graham, *Discovering Images of God: Narratives of Care Among Lesbians and Gays* (Louisville: Westminster John Knox, 1997), 138.

8. Ibid., 113–40.

9. Wilson, *Counseling*, 56.

10. Ibid., 130–40.

11. R. F. Kourany, "Suicide Among Homosexual Adolescents," *Journal of Homosexuality* 13 (4) 111–17.

12. U.S. Department of Health and Human Services, Rockville, Md. (1987), 111–17.

13. Gary Remafedi, James A. Farrow, and Robert Dreisher, "Risk Factors for Attempted Suicide in Gay and Bisexual Youth," Linda Garnets and Douglas Kimmel, *Psychological Perspectives on Lesbian and Gay Male Experiences* (New York: Columbia University Press, 1993), 486–99.

14. For detailed discussions of the pastor's role with suicidal persons, see David K. Switzer, *The Minister as Crisis Counselor* (Nashville: Abingdon, 1986), chapter 9, and *Pastoral Care Emergencies* (Mahwah, N.J.: Paulist, 1989), chapter 8.

15. Mel White, *Stranger at the Gate: To Be Gay and Christian in America* (New York: Simon and Schuster, 1994).

16. American Psychological Association, "Resolution on Treatments to Alter Sexual Orientation," August 14 and 17, 1997. Also on December 11, 1998, the Board of Trustees of the American Psychiatric Association

stated that they oppose "any psychiatric treatment, such as 'reparative' or 'conversion' therapy which is based upon the assumption that homosexuality per se is a mental disorder or . . . that the [person] should change his/her homosexual orientation."

17. Evelyn Hooker, "The Adjustment of the Overt Male Homosexual," *Journal of Projective Techniques* 21 (1957) 18–31.

18. Frederick J. Gaiser, "A New Word on Homosexuality? Isaiah 56:1-8 as a Case Study," *Word and World,* 14/3 (1994). See discussion on pp. 58–60 of this book.

19. William F. Arndt and F. Wilbur Gingrich, *A Greek-English Lexicon of the New Testament* (Chicago: University of Chicago Press, 1957), 699.

20. Scott Hammer, et al., "A Controlled Trial of Two Nucleoside Analogues Plus Indinavir in Persons with Human Immunodeficiency Virus Infection and CD4 Cell Counts of 200 per Cubic Millimeters or Less," *New England Journal of Medicine* 11 (September 1997) 725–33.

21. *Dallas Morning News,* 1997.

22. Switzer, *Pastoral Care Emergencies,* 102.

23. See Further Reading and Resources.

24. Douglas C. Kimmel, "Adult Development and Aging," in Garnets and Kimmel, *Psychological Perspectives,* 520.

25. Linda Garnets, Gregory M. Herek, and Barrie Levy, "Violence and Victimization of Lesbians and Gay Men: Mental Health Consequences," in Garnets and Kimmel, *Psychological Perspectives,* 582.

26. Joretta L. Marshall, *Counseling Lesbian Partners* (Louisville: Westminster John Knox, 1997), 40.

27. Hays, "Awaiting the Redemption," in Siker, *Homosexuality,* 14.

5. PASTORAL CARE AND COUNSELING OF FAMILIES OF GAYS AND LESBIANS

1. For contact information for P-FLAG, see the section on resources for parents in Further Reading and Resources.

2. Jimmy Allen, *Burden of a Secret* (Nashville: Moorings, 1995), 101.

3. Ibid., 102.

4. Ibid.

5. These stages of grief were developed by C. Murray Parkes, "First Year of Bereavement," *Psychiatry* 33 (1970) 448. They are used here with slight modification for the particular circumstances of parents of gays and lesbians. These stages are discussed in a different form and directed to the situations of the parents themselves in David K. Switzer, *Coming Out as Parents: You and Your Homosexual Child* (Louisville: Westminster John Knox, 1996), chapters 1 and 2.

6. W. Robert Beavers, *Psychotherapy and Growth: A Family Systems Perspective* (New York: Brunner/Mazel, 1977), 42–156.

7. See the list of books for parents of gays and lesbians in Further Reading and Resources.

8. "Always Our Children. A Pastoral Message to Parents of Homosexual Children and Suggestions for Pastoral Ministers," *Communications: National Conference of Catholic Bishops/United States Catholic Conference,* Official Press Release, Oct. 1, 1991.

9. Allen, *Burden of a Secret,* 86.

10. Ibid., 127–28.

FURTHER READING AND RESOURCES

BIBLE

Victor Paul Furnish. "Homosexuality." In *The Moral Teaching of Paul: Selected Issues* (revised). Nashville: Abingdon, 1985.

Robin Scroggs. *The New Testament and Homosexuality.* Philadelphia: Fortress, 1983.

PASTORAL CARE

Gerald D. Coleman, S. S. *Homosexuality: Catholic Teaching and Pastoral Practice.* Mahwah, N.J.: Paulist, 1995.

John J. McNeill. "Tapping Deeper Roots: Integrating the Spiritual Dimension into Professional Practice with Lesbian and Gay Clients." *The Journal of Pastoral Care* 48 (Winter 1994) 313–34.

Robert J. Perelli. *Ministry to Persons with AIDS: A Family Systems Approach.* Minneapolis: Augsburg Books, 1991.

Anton Somlais, et al. "An Empirical Investigation of the Relationship Between Spirituality, Coping, and Emotional Distress in People Living with HIV Infection and AIDS." *The Journal of Pastoral Care* 50 (Summer 1996) 151–92.

Ronald Sunderland and Earl E. Shelp. *AIDS: A Manual for Pastoral Care* Philadelphia: Westminster, 1987.

Gail Lynn Unterberger. "Counseling Lesbians: A Feminist Perspective." In Robert J. Wicks and Richard D. Parsons, eds., *Clinical Handbook of Pastoral Counseling,* vol. 2. Mahwah, N.J.: Paulist, 1993; 228–56.

Earl D. Wilson. *Counseling and Homosexuality.* Waco, Tex.: Word Books, 1988.

GENERAL

Jeffrey S. Siker, ed. *Homosexuality in the Church: Both Sides of the Debate.* Louisville: Westminster/John Knox, 1994.

Contains six different topics, with presentations by persons who take different positions on each. Appendix quotes official positions by six denominations.

Marilyn Bennett Alexander and James Preston. *We Were Baptized Too: Claiming God's Grace for Lesbians and Gays.* Louisville: Westminster John Knox, 1996.

FOR PARENTS OF GAYS AND LESBIANS

Betty Fairchild and Nancy Hayward. *Now That You Know: What Every Parent Should Know About Homosexuality.* San Diego: Harcourt Brace Jovanovich, 1986.

Carolyn Welch Griffin, with Marian J. and Arthur G. Wirth. *Beyond Acceptance.* Englewood Cliffs, N.J.: Prentice Hall, 1986.

Contains numerous personal statements by the authors and others concerning their first reactions after discovering that a child was lesbian or gay, and what helped them most. Some references to religion.

David K. Switzer. *Coming Out as Parents: You and Your Homosexual Child.* Louisville: Westminster John Knox, 1996.

The primary emphasis is on parents' various reactions and assisting them in their understanding of what is taking place in their lives and relationships. The role of Christian faith and the support of the church are emphasized.

RESOURCES

AIDS

First, look under AIDS in your local phone book or in that of the nearest larger town or city. Second, call the nearest large hospital and ask about their AIDS services, and if they do not have a specialized program, ask about the nearest hospital that has such services. Third, if no AIDS Interfaith Network can be located, write or call the national office:

National AIDS Interfaith Network
1400 I Street, N.W. Suite 1220
Washington D.C. 20005
(202) 842-0010

They could also direct you to specific national denominational programs.

Parents

If you live in or near a city, look in the city phone book under P-FLAG or Parents and Friends of Lesbians and Gays. If you cannot find such a listing, the national office is 1012 14th Street, N.W., Suite 700, Washington D.C. 20005, phone (202) 638-4200. They might be able to help you find a group near you or offer other helpful suggestions. Also, look under your church denomination's name in the phone book. Some of them in cities will have a group.